Vah,
Mea
child

Reader Reviews

nice!
-Justin

"I can't put it down it is so good. That is a huge compliment considering it's been years since I have read a whole book." - Ruth

"Inspirational at worst, and life changing at best, Justin is committed to seeing Childlike faith lived out among God's people." - David

"In a time when we're so consumed by other people's stories, this book is a breath of fresh air! It beautifully captures how to rediscover your own childlike wonder to live the STORY God wants to write through your life." - Laura

"The Childlike Heist" challenged my dull adult life to be more wonder-filled as I opened my eyes in faith and the hope of seeing Heaven on Earth." - Chelsey

"Justin is whimsical, imaginative and existential in his work as he captures the true heart of wonder. He is able to take our stories and create profound application to the word of God..." - Geordy

Vahan & Vaughn,
May this book inspire your
children to reach their goals!
-Justin

JUSTIN WIESINGER

the Childlike Heist

RECAPTURING CHILDLIKE WONDER
IN A CRAZY MESSED UP ADULT WORLD

YAIRUS
PUBLISHING
HOUSE

YAIRUS Publishing House
www.yairus.com

2   9

FIRST PRINT EDITION
Copyright © 2019 JUSTIN WIESINGER
All rights reserved.

LIBRARY AND ARCHIVES CANADA DATA
ISBN: 978-1-989456-03-3

Editor 1: Ramona Jaggard
Editor 2: Christine Stobbe
Cover Design: Tyler McIntyre
Illustrations: Tyler McIntyre
Interior Formating: Daylon C. Clark

Dedication

To Mark & Sue Wiesinger & family. We lost Josh to this world too soon, but his childlike faith will surely live on in all of us forever.

Table of Contents

Foreword

From its very conception, Justin pulled this effervescent book from his core. This meant vulnerability paved with an inspiring zest for recapturing childlike wonder. True to his nature, as Justin crystallized his thoughts on a page, a bland office just wouldn't do; especially when close to home was a mall, and in this mall lay a pirate ship.

For a season, Justin chronicled the personal revival of his inner lost boy aboard this ship, transforming the monolith from a childlike blip which brushed a tourist's day into something he actively inhabited. Naturally, reclaiming the childlike was contagious. As a loyal contender for the success of others, Justin reimagined the ship while tapping into his array of directing skills to shoot a music video for his friend and local artist, Paul Woida. They crammed hundreds of people into the shoot, and many more saw the project unfold. You see, love always looks like something—and it always overflows. Justin's magnetic personality and lifestyle portray this faithfully.

I have so many stories and memories of Justin where childlike faith and wonder collide, but one memory which stands out in my mind is when Justin accompanied my wife and I to Kenya with Soul Edge Ministries in 2013, when he served as one of our young leaders in training. We had pounded our way with Land Rovers through unforgiving terrain for hundreds of kilometres, incurring numerous flat tires pierced from long cacti needles all in order to reach the heart of a desert region in Northern Kenya called Turkana. We made this journey with a single purpose in mind: to show a largely forgotten tribal people the love of Jesus, both through meeting tangible needs and through ministry.

We stopped in particular villages to set up a medical station, as well as handing out food to families who struggled to find their next meal. On one particular morning, I was on the medical team, and Justin was on our prayer team. As the morning progressed, more and more people began to gather, asking for help. Emerging from the crowd, an older gentleman made his way toward us. I couldn't help but notice how badly crippled he was, bent over from what appeared to have been polio. He came to our medical team and asked if we could do anything. Through translators, we communicated with sadness, though there was nothing we could do for him medically, but our prayer team would love to pray for him. I watched as the man made his way over to Justin and another one of our leaders. He was greeted with a smile from Justin, and I watched as they both laid hands on him. Only moments later, everyone was looking in shock as this man's back began to become straight again. It was hard to believe what was happening. Before they knew it, the man threw down his stick in celebration. Everyone was cheering and Justin's face said it all. A massive smile sprang up across his face! That evening, beneath the manifold glory of the starlit heavens, we celebrated like crazy, dancing with the village because of all those who had been healed by Jesus. I will never forget seeing this particular healed man jumping in worship and giving thanks to God: totally healed, back straight. Complete, infectious Joy was his testimony!

For many of us, if we were confronted with this kind of situation, we would have fallen into doubt and maybe even fear, but Justin prayed with such a beautiful confidence and faith in who his heavenly Father was. This truth changes everything; all around the world, as sons and daughters of God lay hold of this earth-shattering truth it changes lives forever.

I think back to a conversation Jesus had with his disciples. They once asked Him, "Who will be the greatest in the Kingdom?"

I have always been stunned by Jesus' answer: He doesn't rebuke them for asking the question. Instead, He brings a child into their midst and says, "If you want to be great, you need to become like a child." Essentially, the way of the Kingdom of God requires us to walk in a childlike posture of radical trust and wonder. Justin was always an adventurer, but now his wandering had purpose and clear vision. Jesus had utterly captivated his heart and there was no going back.

May you be blessed, as we have been to know Justin, as you journey to recapture childlike wonder.

Josh and Kiri Erb
Directors of Soul Edge Ministries

JUSTIN WIESINGER

the
Childlike
Heist

RECAPTURING CHILDLIKE WONDER
IN A CRAZY MESSED UP ADULT WORLD

ONE

The Roll Reversal

I used to think to be childlike was a season to life.
Now I know that it is the point of life.

I can still remember when I drove my parent's car for the first time. I was three years old. Other than my sister's recounting of this story, I feel I only remember this predicament due to the impending scolding from my father hours later.

My mother was taking my nine-year-old sister Janice and me out for an afternoon errand run to the grocery store and the mall. She left her car keys in the ignition and quickly ran back inside to grab her purse and use the washroom. Leaving the keys was a big mistake on her part. This whole ordeal kick-started with my wide-eyed, childish curiosity. I couldn't help but be captivated by my mother's 1986 Chevrolet Station Wagon. This baby was one of those cars with the glossy wooden panel siding. There was enough trunk space in this flashy car to transport a grand piano or two.

I stared at the leather-wrapped steering wheel with my mouth wide open in sheer fascination. Each time my mother spun the wheel to the right and left, my head turned side to side in a rhythmic trance. I desperately longed for the moment I could get behind the wheel of that car and take it for a joyride.

By this time in my preschool journey, I had mustered up enough courage to try this driving activity out for myself. I recall quickly climbing out of my unbuckled car seat to sit behind the wheel. My sister wasn't too concerned because she knew I didn't know how to start the vehicle. But what she didn't realize was that I knew how to change the gear shifter.

I had seen my mother swing that gear shift a million times, so I gripped it with my right hand and yanked it downward, slipping the car into neutral. The car was parked midway up the hill of our driveway, so it slowly began to roll backward down the lane. A broad smile widened across my rosy cheeks as I got the car into full motion. My sister was not jiving with this whole moving-in-reverse idea and began to scream. She didn't know what to do and didn't have the guts to hop out of the car and get help. She just sat in the back seat like a champ, pounding on the windows and yelling for dear life.

Luckily, there were no other cars in our immediate vicinity. Nor were any neighbours around to witness this royal parenting fail. After several seconds of constant shrieking from the backseat, my sister had finally had enough. She lunged toward the driver's dash and grabbed the gear shifter out of my tiny hands. Janice managed to shove it back into park which brought the massive town car to a halt in the middle of the street.

It's a miracle my sister and I were not hurt, though I'm sure she felt emotionally scarred from the ordeal. Somehow, I learned my lesson from that situation. I decided it was a good idea to wait at least a year or two before trying that stunt again. I stuck to my training wheels on the bike and scooter in the interim.

Looking back on that fond memory now, it's funny to think about how I was so fascinated with that less-than-classy vehicle. I was desperate to drive it. That old car mesmerized me, and my childlike mind viewed this station wagon as a motorized miracle. I had this brilliant, carefree curiosity about how this car came to be, and wondered whose mind this grand invention unfolded from.

I think a three-year-old treats everything in life as if it's a miracle. Children at this age are constantly smelling, tasting, touching, and keeping their eyes peeled for the presence of magic and wonder. I heard someone say how children believe there are a million wonders in the world, not just a measly seven. William Yeats, an Irish poet, once wrote how "the world is full of magical things patiently waiting for our senses to grow sharper." Growing up is conducive to weakening our awareness of the miraculous around us. Our lives are a miracle, and we should treat them as such every day. When our childlike wonder wears thin, our lives grow old and dull as a result.

I often wonder if our adult selves are missing out on a large part of the beauty and wonder of life. It would be a shame to journey through a lifetime and miss out on truly living. It's as if children are living in an alternate reality, or a different kingdom entirely.

I believe we are all born living in the kingdom of heaven, but sooner or later we forget about it along the way or grow out of it as we grow up into adults. The Bible says that God has written eternity into the hearts of men. Jesus says that His kingdom is at hand; it's not distant or too far away to reach us. This eternal kingdom beckons our childlike selves onward and upward into the far-reaching emerald islands, into the rainbow-chalk-covered highways and byways of curiosity, into the imaginative lands of whimsy, wonder, and fascination. The beauty of this kingdom is plastered to every wall of our childhood imaginations, as we learn to play and dream up other realities in our minds.

It's easy to miss the wonder and magic of this life when the modern education systems indoctrinate us at an early age. Teachers often try to keep our lessons fun and engaging, but our childlike creativity takes a hit when we are taught to conform to tough guidelines and to think a certain way in school. Each pop quiz and test is another fatal blow to our childlike nature. Our colouring books grow dustier the more we are taught to colour inside the lines. Schools wear away our God-given creative legacy until every student's childlike mind fades and corrodes. Our curiosity for the wonder of this life is slowly replaced with boring textbooks and regurgitated information. We only have what we can remember, and soon the remembrance of heaven's wonder is replaced with piles of homework and countless assignments.

The world starts lying to us from a very young age that things aren't all that remarkable or magical anymore. The world perpetuates the lie early on that we have to wait until we're all 'grown up' before we can be useful and fulfill our childhood dreams. The news reporters and scientists explain to children that life is an assortment of random events with minimal significance. It's as if the gates of the kingdom of heaven are boarded up and overshadowed by brick mortar walls of theories, rational equations, and the thoughts of appropriated adulthood.

I believe deep down that this life is both miraculous and remarkable in every possible way. There's a war going on for our souls, and it starts when we are children.

The apostle Paul wrote in one of his letters how when he became a man, he chose to put aside his childish ways and leave them behind. This is a vital lesson we can learn from, but I think many of us have misinterpreted and confused this scripture in our own lives. Though Paul doesn't say anything about putting away our childlike ways, such as our God-given creativity, imagination, dreams, and wonder. He is telling us to put aside childish ways such as complaining, name calling, unforgiveness, and anger.   We can so easily fall into the trap of believing that we need to put aside our childlikeness, and grow up. Many of us even think that it's Biblical, or the christian thing to do, but it's certainly not. One of the greatest lies the enemy has us believe is that being childlike is a sin, or downright irresponsible of us. Much of our religious culture propitiates this same sentiment, leaving us feeling stagnant, indifferent, and bored in our daily lives.

This twisted view of reality causes us to stay parked in our lives, just like that station wagon was parked in the driveway. I think God is beckoning us to be curious like children and to throw that car in reverse. It's vital to know that the childlike self is our truest self, and we can all access this part of us again if we choose to.

As we roll back into the memories of our child-hoods, we will discover the childlike wonder hiding inside all of us. Our childlike self, who is still full of whimsy and adventure, is just waiting to get the car rolling again.

This magnificent event of rolling backwards down

the driveway of our lives, back into our childhoods, will help us rediscover our childlike self that's been in hiding. You might even find yourself screaming like my sister did as you begin to reminisce about your broken childhood. We aren't travelling back to those moments to just remember. We are journeying back to those moments to learn, to heal, and to rediscover the wonders of childlike faith again. It's far too damaging to stay in park when we have a marvellous life of adventure awaiting us. We can be certain that it's this childlike spirit which has the power to change the world forever.

I think a lot of people have this faulty idea that their lives are in full motion when really they're standing still. I think we can all confuse a lot of activity, busyness, or even a perfect church attendance with truly living. Jesus never asked us to only agree with His teachings while we sit planted in the rows of church pews, or as we listen to sermons on the radio. He asks us to take a risk by stepping out in childlike faith and following His lead wherever that may take us.

So many people are obsessed with their retirements. Jesus never encouraged us to take a vacation or an early retirement from the incredible life He offers us. Jesus never promoted acting like a 'grown up' either.

Many of us get old in our thinking and mistakingly act our age as we grow older. Acting our age is merely a faulty mindset we can let go of. We are only as old as we think we are. We can trick our adult minds into feeling young at heart forever. You are never too old to embrace a life of meaning and adventure. You are never too old to let go of these limiting beliefs and moving into unchartered territory of wonder. The childlike mindset dictates that we are never old enough to retire.

Jesus calls us all onward and upward into a life of adventure and magical discovery. Jesus knows that many of us won't understand moving forward until we catch a glimpse of His majestic kingdom in the rearview mirror. It's the very kingdom we grew out of along the way and left behind in the driveways of our lives. Though it might be scary, and you might even terrify a few passengers or friends in the process, Jesus promises us it will be worth it in the end.

Maybe you've had some tough seasons or challenging setbacks in your lifetime. We can't let a few speed bumps and screams scare us out of risking a life of adventure and wonder. Going in reverse might not make sense right at the start, but Jesus will help clarify this less-travelled road along the way. Reminiscing and healing from our childhood hurts will help us journey closer with Jesus. Walking side by side with Him is where He always planned for us to be. Jesus said how we'd discover this kingdom in the places we'd least expect. I began to rediscover this remarkable kingdom while laughing with my sister about this ridiculous three-year-old grand theft auto caper.

It's time to recapture a part of your childlike self which is begging to come out and play. It's time to look for the magic of the kingdom of heaven again, which lies hostage and dormant inside all of us. It's hiding in plain sight, right near the gear shifter of our fears. We must summon the courage to move our lives from park into reverse, trusting that Jesus has the wheel.

I still believe in miracles, because after all of my mess-ups and shortcomings, Jesus still believes in me.

TWO

All Aboard the
Imagination Station

I used to think I had to be a preacher to get into heaven.
Now I know being childlike gets heaven into me.

My family often made the lengthy trek across the Saskatchewan prairies to visit my relatives in that dusty neighbouring province. Saskatchewan is flat: people say if you lost your dog there, you'd be able to see it run away for a week.

We would often stop in at Uncle Mark's acreage when en route to my grandpa and grandma's home in Yorkton. He lived on a beautiful farm a half-hour south of Saskatoon. My cousins and I got up to all kinds of mischief at my uncle's house.

I'm blessed to say I come from a fairly large and crazy family. I have eighteen first cousins on my father's side. My uncle Mark had five children of his own. We had numerous fond capers together, which involved riding turkeys bareback around the yard, ninja boxing matches, and sleeping under the stars on their giant trampoline.

I'm certain my parents prayed fervently before taking my sister and me on long road trips to Saskatche-wan. They desperately needed a solution to the fierce quarrelling and elastic band shooting matches between my sister and me on the long drives.

When I was four years old, I believe an angel spoke to my father in a dream and gave him a majestic solution to all the road trip troubles. He bought my first cassette tape of Adventures in Odyssey. If you grew up in a God-fearing home in the 90s, as I did, this radio play series was the pinnacle of a parent's dream of childhood pacification, without the necessity of using any major sedatives in their children's grapefruit juice. Listening to Odyssey was a great way to pass the time on those long trips. This program was my parent's favourite method to get me to fall asleep.

My mother would tuck me into bed and slide in the cassette tape and hit play. The old familiar theme song swelled up as Corey, the announcer, introduced each fantastic episode. Hitting play on the old tape deck took my imagination through a portal to another dimension. I don't even think I fell asleep those nights listening to those Odyssey tapes; I fell into an entirely different world.

Each episode was packed with adventure, intrigue, suspense, life lessons, and discovery. It's enough to encourage a preschooler to wet his bed out of overexcite-ment. (Not that this happened to me, though!) If there is ever a way to fuel your imagination as a youngster, this program was the golden nugget equivalent of perfection.

Mr. Whittaker was one of my favourite characters in the radio drama. He was a wise man, with an endearing touch of whimsy about him, yet he was mysterious as well. Whit was an artisan, a seasoned inventor who owned the largest kid-friendly wonder emporium and ice cream parlour in town. This marvellous place was called Whit's

Whit's imagination was large enough to swallow entire worlds into his fantastic, creative universe. He gave me so much hope as a young child. I aspired to be just like him when I was old enough to grow white whiskers and talk funny with a crackle of wisdom in my voice.

There is something amazing about the way Mr. Whittaker engaged in conversation and life with children of all ages. He never passed judgements or gave them a list of harsh rules to follow. He had a keen passion in his heart to see every child who ever walked into his ice cream shop become something amazing.

Children and youth from all over the town of Odyssey flocked to Whit's End because they knew they would be safe and encouraged to be children again, or at least to act like it. As I listened night after night to those familiar episodes, I felt like I was right there, caught up in the wonder of each unfolding story.

Mr. Whittaker even created a time machine called the "Imagination Station." This incredible machine would allow youngsters to escape into different times, places, and realities. The children would visit the birth of a nation, Joan of Arc, the underground railroad, or be caught in the thick of the action of real Bible stories. As a wise 1980's professor once said: "Where we're going we don't need roads." The characters kissed Odyssey goodbye with the flip of a shiny switch.

My happy times in Odyssey helped me to block out the not-so-fond events in my childhood. On one occasion, in the middle of the night, my mother fainted in the hallway while returning from the washroom. I happened to be awake and saw her fall to the ground with a loud thud outside my room. It's not easy for a six-year-old to watch his mother get carried out of their home on a stretcher by firefighters and emergency workers. I stood there shaking, crying in wide-eyed terror, wondering if I would ever see my mother alive again. I didn't find out what had happened to her until the next morning. She was okay, but she took a hard fall.

Like this incident with my mother falling, there were many images of pain and fear from my childhood attempting to reflect their images back onto me. My early childhood of innocence and wonder resembled a shiny mirror; untainted and glimmering with childlike purity and curiosity. The clear vision and reflection of who God had made me to be as a child became foggy over time, with each mishap, failure, and heartache along the way.

Despite these challenging times, I still had my own imagination station to make my grand, all-too-frequent escape to another world, a world I created in my heart, where nobody could hurt me, or yell at me, or discourage me from my God-sized dreams.

I think we often underestimate the power of the human imagination. We too often fall into the trap of needing things to be rational and realistic in our human experiences. It's hard to justify what we can't quantify with solid facts and equations. Wayne Dyer, an American philosopher, said "Everything that now exists was once imagined So, if you want something to exist, you must be able to imagine it."

There's a blurred line between our imaginations and the reality we see in front of us. It is evident that what we focus on and imagine becomes our reality around us. We could learn a thing or two from the little children running around us who use their imaginations unceasing-

Whenever I read stories of Jesus in the Bible, He reminds me of Mr. Whittaker. Jesus would often call for the little children to come to Him, to draw close to their Father. It must have given Jesus much joy to see those little world-changers living out their childlike faith and wonder in the presence of their creator. These children didn't need to listen to a sermon to believe Jesus was who He claimed to be. They needed to hear His voice, run to His open arms, and jump on His lap in complete trust and childlike abandon.

I don't think Jesus ever intended for us to grow out of wanting to jump up on His lap and enjoy His presence. If I'm honest, I've been guilty of growing up at times and growing out of needing Jesus close by my side. I now know there's a better path for us which Jesus calls us to, and it requires our inner child to come out and play again.

Inside my heart lives a six-year-old who is steadily lost in the depths of his imagination. The only difference now is I have begun to learn the true power of what Jesus calls us to do with this incredible, limitless, mental faculty. I've been using my imagination lately to envision a better world; a world where I can play my part in helping make things better for those around me.

I've been learning lately how our lives are made up of our most prominent thoughts and our most permeated dreams. Our imagination is the playground of heaven where our wildest dreams and our greatest hopes can become reality around us.

A memorable proverb states the following: As a man thinks in his heart, so he becomes. If our hearts are the fertile soil of heaven's garden, what are we choosing to plant? What is growing in the soil of our lives? Are we growing a childlike dream, or have our grown up anxieties grown like thistles and weeds, slowly choking out heaven's kingdom perspective?

Many of us have lost the courage to dream huge God-sized dreams. People of all ages are forgetting what it's like to imagine a better world or a better life.

Imagination is the fire that fuels the soul. We must never let it burn out! The loss of our imagination jeopardizes our ability to allow our inner child to thrive amidst life's setbacks and challenges.

I want to see the people around me growing the courage to pick up the broken pieces of their childhoods, embrace childlike wonder, and truly dream again. There's a world of wonder waiting to be excavated and explored in our own backyards. We need to pray for the courage and faith to see it.

Jesus spoke of how we wouldn't be able to see this imaginative world with our human eyes, but rather with our childlike hearts. This magical kingdom is hiding in plain view, right behind our mortgages, car payments and retirement funds. It's brightening up the darkest of alleyways with rainbows and balloons. This marvellous world is drowning out the noises of busyness with joy and laughter. It's filling up the hospitals and prisons with songs of hope and freedom. It's slowly shaking the very foundations of the systems of this world, which are attempting to keep our childlike wonder caged in and locked away.

It's my hope and prayer we would all grow to learn and understand the pain of our youth and the struggles in this life have a purpose. Jesus is the only one who can bring true redemption and meaning to our heavy hearts. Jesus is the purpose we can call on for help in the midst of the turmoil of this messy, crazy life.

This carpenter-turned-rabbi named Jesus made the audacious claim He was the Son of God. He spoke quite a few epic one-liners in His short time here on earth, too. His Twitter feed would have blown up overnight if He was online today. He once said the kingdom of heaven is at hand, it's here right now. Jesus also spoke of how we needed to become like little children to see and enter the kingdom of heaven. He said it's as close as our own skin.

It seems like a lot of adults who claim to follow Jesus refuse to acknowledge this kingdom of heaven, or are too busy doing their own thing to stop and see it being built up around them. We too often get so busy doing church and Christian things, our pride and need for independence gets in the way of us encountering childlike faith. It's like we grow up to the point we grow out of needing Jesus in our lives. We choose to believe the wonder and beauty of childlikeness are reserved for a season of our life called childhood. This kingdom Jesus calls us to is not reserved only for children. God's plan for all of us is to grow young again in our faith and the ways we approach God's kingdom reality.

It takes the faith of a child to enter this kingdom which is so different than our world today. I think the present-day church often confuses the idea of "childlike faith" with "childish faith." There's a big discrepancy between being childish and being childlike.

I want to paint a vivid picture of Jesus for you from the perspective of childlike faith and wonder. Let's use our imaginations and dream up a better world together. Let's escape on an adventure, to find our childlike selves who have been hiding in the shadows for far too long. Something ignites hope and joy inside me when I hear the simple words coming from the mouth of Jesus. It's like He's sitting behind the counter at Whit's End, with a mysterious twinkle in His eye, pouring another chocolate milkshake, saying, "Want to come and see the imagination station?"

THREE

The Power to Break the Ice

I used to think we had to say a prayer to meet Jesus.
But now I know sometimes we meet him by surprise.

Every kid has a defining moment in their childhood, when a parent blows their little minds by allowing them to partake in a new and exciting experience. My next story is not for the faint of heart. Sometimes I have to pinch my five-year-old self to ensure this happened the way I remember.

The first father-son date of my childhood was one for the record books. I was five years old and was a fireball of energy and enthusiasm. The intrigue of this evening out with my father was he didn't offer many details; he kindly encouraged me to go with him for some pizza. After our delicious meal, and with cheese string still freshly stuck to my chin; we jumped back into my father's truck. On the way to our destination, my father let a few vital details slip out. He mentioned swords, fire, and smashing things with bare muscles. Where do I sign up?

We pulled up to the old Central Tabernacle in downtown Edmonton. The building was shaped like a pyramid, and I vividly recall how the building was covered brown, sun-worn roofing shingles. As we approached the foyer, I noticed numerous other boys strolling in with their fathers. We all had the same awestruck look on our faces; a look of expectancy and trepidation all rolled into one. The show hadn't even started yet, and we were already drunk on adrenaline.

I recall a large banner encircling the entrance which read "THE POWER TEAM" in punchy, red, Karate-Kid-meets-Jackie-Chan-styled letters. I felt like we were back in the Roman civilization, filing into the Coliseum, preparing our untainted eyes for unthinkable bloodshed and carnage.

My father and I took our seats as the lights dimmed low. The audience fell silent. The pastor introduced the performers as the sound guys cued some epic 1980's rock music. Then suddenly, out of one of the stage wings, a large, muscular man with long, flowing, blonde hair hulked his way out onto the stage. I didn't know guys as fit as him were allowed to have long, beautiful hair like that.

Throughout the evening, the performers engaged in one crazy feat of strength after another. The mighty men ripped giant phone books in half with their bare hands. One guy swung a sword around like Braveheart in the thick of battle. They hoisted weights over their heads which could grind an ordinary man's spine down to powder.

The crowd of wide-eyed observers emitted constant cries of "ooh" and "ahhh." The testosterone-laden audience were in a rhythmic trance. This was an unforgettable celebration of everything manly and dangerous.

I attended a visual buffet of awesomeness that night; every kid went up for thirds and fourths, until we imagined our biceps grew noticeably larger. Little did we know, but all of these feats of power were a gradual build up, preparing our wonder-filled eyes for the grand finale.

At the end of the show, the entire Power Team came out on stage, flexed their muscles one last time, and made their formal bows to the audience. If these burly men had been Roman gladiators, they would have easily slain every lion and chariot rider in the ring. Every kid and father in the auditorium erupted in mighty shouts and battle cries. I even saw a few fathers throw their youngest sons in the air, in a proud, Lion King sort of moment. An older gentleman further down from us began to sob, as though reminiscing about his childhood.

After the cheering subsided, we took our seats, and the Power Team announcer came out on stage. He quietly explained, "We have one final, extremely dangerous and exhilarating feat of strength for you gentlemen this evening. I'm going to have to invite the pastor of Central Tabernacle up to the stage."

The spectators put their hands together and welcomed the tall and comparatively skinny, frail- looking minister to the stage. The lights dimmed down again, and a spotlight exploded onto the pastor. Another strong man wheeled out a blanket-covered table. The announcer asked the pastor to take his shirt off and explained everything was going to be okay.

Then suddenly, before I could properly comprehend what was going on, they peeled back the blanket on the cart to reveal a bed of nails! The announcer explained the pastor should lie down on his back on top of the nails. A building chatter billowed out amongst the audience. Boys all over the room were asking their fathers if it's a normal occurrence for pastors in their later years to seek a quick ticket to heaven.

I glanced up at my father in fear. I was shaking under the intensity of the situation. He slowly put his arm around me and motioned for me to look forward. As terrified as I felt in that moment, it's like my father was saying it's going to be okay. I stared at the violent display unfolding before me.

The pastor lay down across the sheet of nails, and hundreds of sharp nail pricks poked into his back. Any sudden movement such as a sneeze or a cough would have sent him to the hospital. The announcer then placed a towel across the pastor's chest. I couldn't get a good look at the poor pastor's face, though I'm certain he was saying his final prayers and sending love to his wife and children.

As if it couldn't get any more surreal and terrifying, another Hulk Hogan look-alike wheeled out a second cart bearing a giant, square brick of ice. It must have weighed sixty pounds! This muscular menace picked up the block of ice and placed it on the pastor's chest.

Another masculine star of the show came out wielding a hefty sledgehammer. This unfolding scene began to play out in my tiny mind in slow motion. I think every kid in the room came to the same conclusion as I did. They all wanted desperately to do something to save this innocent, frail-looking man.

Though this was painful to watch first hand, I decided to trust my father, who assured me it's all going to play out okay in the end. Everyone keenly focused as the announcer made a quick analogy about God and about the enemy being defeated. He said how Jesus had laid down his life for humanity, like this pastor lay down on this bed of nails. The brick of ice represented our sin and separation from God. Jesus bore the weight of the sins of the world while he hung nailed to a cross. The passionate announcer then lifted up his giant hammer and said, "But nothing could separate us from the love of our heavenly Father."

Smoke began to billow onto the stage as a courageous song swelled up and filled the sanctuary. The announcer shouted, "And with one final blow, Jesus swallowed the grave!"

The sledgehammer made its abrupt descent toward its helpless victim and slammed into the ice with an earth-shattering impact. It sounded like a semi-truck slamming into a grand piano on the highway. I imagined shards of cold, ice shrapnel shooting off in every direction, forcing the crowd in the first few rows to dive and duck for cover. The impact, like a barrage of bullets, would rip chunks of wood off the pews! I still don't know how my father sat there so calmly. Maybe he came prepared in a Kevlar vest. Maybe he fought during the Korean War and knew the risks involved. Or maybe all of the dads were only trying to look tough!

As the mist of ice dissolved from the air, a few of the boys were coughing and rolling on the floor, as if recovering from a nearby mortar blast. This crazy scene played out like we were deep in the Amazon jungles, precariously enshrouded in the terrifying, heartless trenches of war.

When the ringing in my ears finally dissipated, I shook off the shock of the event and came to my senses. The other boys and I quietly peeked out of our imaginary trenches, gazing overtop of the church pews, with a clear view of the casualty off in the distance.

The pastor's body was still intact. There were no

signs of open wounds, bleeding, or lacerations of any kind. All of a sudden, the pastor slowly arose from the bed of nails. He began to move his head and limbs. He was alive! The announcer then grabbed the pastor's hand and hoisted it up in the air as they faced the audience. Our young, childlike minds did all of the mental calculations for how this could have played out, but we had never anticipated this miraculous victory.

What a glorious picture had been painted before our eyes! When on the surface, it looked like all the odds were stacked against him, somehow, someway, this pastor cheated death and never felt the sting of it.

I'm still not quite sure if I felt raw emotions, the hugs from complete strangers, or the short story which the announcer shared that stirred excitement in my heart. Adrenaline was coursing through my veins, and my heart was pounding in my chest. I couldn't help but ponder the idea how death had been defeated. The notion of us being more than conquerors through Christ was like a bell ringing on the inside of me.

I saw God's love on display for the first time in my life, in the form of a lanky pastor lying on a bed of nails. This analogy reminded me of the lengths Jesus took to ensure we would have a new life with Him forever. He didn't want a world without a relationship with us, and He would do whatever it took to ensure we would get to be with Him one day. Jesus knew He had to take the bed of nails called the cross to pay for our sins. It wasn't easy, but in the end, the price was worth the reward.

Unlike the pastor, these nails pierced Jesus' hands and feet all the way through. Thankfully, though, this isn't how the story ended. Jesus conquered the grave so none of us would feel the sting of death. His victory became our victory, too. We are truly now more than conquerors through Christ who first loved us and gave Himself for us. Just the thought of Jesus kicking death's butt carried a lot of firepower!

If this is the truth—Jesus defeated death on our behalf—then surely this changes everything. It means we can stop picking fights with our neighbours, school bullies, and neighbouring countries. I bet all of these wars and rumours of wars we hear about on the news could go up in a puff of icy smoke, with one inexplicable act of fearless love.

There is something so courageous, so bold, so uncanny about the notion of conquering death itself. I didn't know a lot about Jesus at a young age, but I sure wanted to spend the rest of my life finding out about this loving, death-crushing hero.

The imagery of Jesus demolishing sin and death like the smashing of the hefty block of ice spoke to me of what Jesus did for us on Calvary.

As my father and I made our way out of the auditorium, a piece of merchandise caught my attention. I froze in amazement.

"Justin, Justin!" my father blurted out. "Do you want this white Power Team bandana?" The bandana was red and white, with bold, ninja-like lettering which read: POWER. I quickly nodded my head. The bandana was a treasured keepsake of mine, with which I had many grand adventures playing ninjas and bad guys for countless hours with my neighbourhood friends. This bandana held the key to unlocking one of my fondest childhood memories.

I keep a treasure chest of childhood trinkets and memorabilia in my old room at my parents' place. I recall rummaging around the room several years ago, packing for a summer camp job, when I stumbled upon the old red and white bandana. As I held the worn fabric in my hands, this awesome memory jolted back to the forefront of my mind. I recalled what it's like to be a kid and to go on an adventure with my father.

I reflected on my encounter with Jesus that fateful evening, as I sat beside my father taking in the experience. I'm so thankful for the remarkable image of redemption, watching the Power Team all of those years ago. Somewhere between the muscles, ice, and smoke, I met Jesus for the first time, and it changed the course of my life forever.

A few summers ago, I tied the old bandana around my head, and knew I wanted to create some remarkable memories of God's love for the campers I would be leading all summer. I stopped at a promising garage sale on the way to camp and purchased a replica Braveheart sword from the movie. I didn't yet have a formal plan for how I was going to make this summer memorable for the kids, but I knew it would involve a weekly knighting ceremony. Each week, I would encourage the youngsters to begin their own adventures with Jesus, and in doing so, make the moment stick in their memories forever.

Sometimes it can feel like a block of ice has frozen over our favourite childhood memories. This block of ice can resemble taking adulthood far too seriously, but I think a lot of it resembles forgetting the moments which defined us with wonder as kids.

It's easy to want to ignore the painful moments of

our younger years, but with choosing to overlook those hard times, a few of our fond memories are forgotten too. We are left feeling cold, callous, and forgetful of the childlike moments which shaped us when we were young. If we forget who we were, it becomes all too easy to forget who we are becoming, too.

Maybe you were introduced to Jesus as a kid, but somehow this moment is frozen in a thick block of ice somewhere between your first heartache and the first time you felt rejected at school. Jesus holds the sledgehammer to help us chip away at the ice blocks crushing our childlike selves. It's time to dig out some old family photos or stored away toys to jog your memory. I know none of this story would have jumped to the forefront of my mind without a helpful, bandana- sized reminder.

Let's regain the childlike courage and the strength which gives us the power to break the ice over our eventful childhoods. Those memories are too precious to leave trapped frozen in time. Sharing these stories with others could be a doorway to breakthrough and discovery in their own lives.

Every time we remember vital memories from our past, where our inner child roamed free, it reveals another glimpse of the story God is painting in our lives. We aren't characters in a weekly sitcom living out random episodes and scenes. Our lives resemble a movie; we get to learn from our past and ask Jesus who we are becoming along the way. Let's ask Him for the strength to pick up this massive sledgehammer and get down to business with the block of ice immobilizing our childhood. We owe it to ourselves to remember.

FOUR

Buying Batman

I used to think Jesus was boring,
but now I know He's more like Batman.

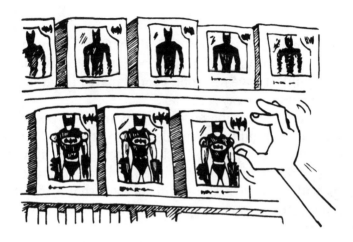

I was never allowed to own action hero figures in my early years. At least, not the ones which promoted butt-kicking or violence. There were a few Winnie The Pooh plastic characters in my play cabinet, not to mention my immense reservoir of Lego pieces.

I would often quickly change the channel on our ancient television set to sneak in some epic Saturday morning action-hero cartoons. I had this whole ingenious switch down to a science. Tricking my parents from time to time was the sort of science I could really get behind.

The superhero cartoons made me marvel at how seemingly ordinary people could make a huge impact on the world. I was astounded when I found out Batman didn't have any real superhuman powers. He was well connected, came from a wealthy family, and had an undying passion and commitment to his cause. Bruce Wayne had every excuse to be afraid of the dark, and of scary bats, for that matter. But instead, he chose to embrace his fears and face them head-on. Bruce would even dress like what he feared to scare the bad guys of Gotham City. The reality of who Batman was and what he stood for ignited a spark in me as a child. It gave me hope I could match his greatness in my own unique way someday.

One fateful Friday evening, my mother was taking my six-year-old self to Toys R Us for the first time. It must be so exciting for parents to blow their little children's minds by taking them to new places and experiencing new things with them. I had a slight idea of what a toy store was, but nothing could prepare me for this mega toy store adventure.

I was giddy on the car ride to the toy store, as I asked my mother what to expect. My sights were laser-focused on finding my own Batman action figure. My imagination sprang to life, with the thought of the towering walls of action figures and the giant boxes of lego sets.

I still vividly remember the dim lights in the parking lot and the scattered cars strewn about, as if the mall was nearly closed. As we drove around a corner, light began to pour onto the hood of the car, almost blinding me. I tried my best to make out what the sign said. I read a T, and an R—Toys R Us! I was now drawing ever closer to leaving the store with the Dark Knight in my hands.

We slowly walked into the massive store while my mother gave me explicit instructions to stay close by her side. Those were the days of the awkward mother-son hand-holding scenario, or the whole-purse grab.

My mother continued to ramble off some instructions as she guided me through the store. My beady little eyes were completely mesmerized by the layout of the building. The shelves on the aisles must have measured two miles high. The stacks of toys on the shelves must have numbered in the hundreds of millions. I could have tried counting all the Buzz Lightyears in the store, but would have failed to finish due to dying from frustration or starvation. This toy store knew how to do things right. They should have called the store Toys R Everywhere!

I quickly abandoned my mother in the store after her sincere, heartfelt debrief. My heart was pounding through my chest. I had only seen a few Batman action figures in my short lifetime. It was never enough for me to play with someone else's toys; I had to have my own Batman. I felt like my inner boy radar was going off and leading me to the right aisle as I flowed down the rigid corridors.

I took a right, a left, another right, walked a bit further, then there he was. I stopped dead in my tracks. Bruce Wayne starred right back at me with a look of fearless resolve. This was the turning point of my entire life!

The shiny, plastic packaging enhanced the shimmer and glow of the masked figure. His suit was dark grey, and his glimmering utility belt looked like it had twenty-four karat gold features. He had all the bells and whistles you could ever ask for in a hero. I reached out and carefully clasped the box, being sure not to wake up my new friend, just in case he'd had a long night out beating up Falconie's henchmen. I was utterly speechless.

I glanced to the left and right to make sure no other boys were observing this religious experience. I slowly looked up to the heavens. The blinding fluorescent store lighting stared right back down at me. There was no other option but to take Batman home with me, no matter the cost. I didn't bother to check the price tag. I ran straight to my mother and pulled out all of the stops at once. The glimpse of the Dark Knight clasped in my hands quickly overshadowed her relief at seeing me resurface.

"Mom—umm—this is—let me introduce you to Batman!" I nervously shrieked. My mother shook her head and firmly replied, "I don't think so, Justin. He looks far too scary and dark." My heart sank in disbelief. "But, Mom! He's a really good man!" I enthusiastically pleaded.

Spending the next ten minutes explaining my case to her was worth every ounce of effort. I told her how something tragic happened to Bruce when he was a youngster like me. I explained how his parents were shot in cold blood, and he was forced to grow up and face his fears. He made it his life's purpose to help those who couldn't help themselves—to stand up to the bad guys of Gotham city and fight for justice. She paused for a few moments to take it all in. I knew I had this in the bag. Judge Judy couldn't have made a better case for Batman.

After what seemed like a lifetime of thought, my mother calmly reached down, grabbed my hand, and took me to the checkout. This was awesome! My dream of having my very own masked hero in my room had come to pass. Deep down, I believed if I could convince my mother to let me have my own superhero action figures, I could grow up to be a real-life superhero someday. I had to hang around them long enough to learn their skills, their punching methods, and their best-kept hero secrets.

There are a lot of people who judge others at face value, like my mother deciding at first glance, how Batman was frightening and evil. She didn't know a thing about Batman, nor did she care to find out. All she knew was her biased opinion of him based on his appearance, which was far from the truth.

I know of a real-life superhero who has been misunderstood and thrown under the bus more times than I can count. His name is Jesus, the teacher from Nazareth.

I think all of us have been guilty at one point or another of talking about Jesus behind His back, without ever getting to know Him. We can so easily make assumptions about who He is and what He does based on our 'in the box,' and 'on the shelf' opinions of Him. Sure, we pass by Him from time to time, but we are too often concerned with what others will think of us if we take Him out of the box or take Him home with us.

We never bother to read the fine print on the labels either. We never bother to ask our friends, who know a little bit more about Jesus than we do, what He's really like. We know there are a lot of people who follow Him and take Him out of their religious boxes, out of the shiny plastic packaging.

I don't think Jesus wants us to observe Him on the wall of the toy store aisle anymore. He must be sick and tired of us gossiping about Him, with our limited knowledge and overwhelming hypocrisy. He wants us to take Him off the toy store shelf, remove the shiny religious packaging, and go on crazy adventures with Him and our friends down the street.

Jesus is like Batman. He grew up in a normal family, maybe not as well off as Bruce Wayne's family, but He learned a great deal about caring for others from His earthly parents. He grew up with scars, bruises, and hurts, like all of us. The main thing which separated Jesus from the vast majority of the people of His time, was how He knew what His purpose was on earth. Though the plan for His life was enough to make him sweat blood out of indescribable fear, he trusted the process and died the hero.

There's a quote from a recent Batman movie which explains, "You either die as the hero or live long enough to become the villain."

Like Batman, Jesus managed to make a lot of friends as well as a lot of enemies during His short time here on earth. Some of his close friends even rejected Him and lied to others by saying they never knew Him! He died a criminal's death on the cross and was raised to new life three days later, having conquered death and sin on our behalf. How's that for an action hero story!

Jesus saw the needs of others all around Him, and He showed mercy, compassion, love, and forgiveness. I don't recall any mention of Him sitting in coffee shops whining to his friends about all of the horrible things going on in the world. I don't recall Jesus being a small group leader, telling people the right things to believe. He was a go-getter; a doer. Jesus was never too full of Himself to offer love and compassion to those around Him. He fought for those who were powerless to fight for themselves.

Maybe Jesus didn't run around at night in a cape and cowl. Maybe He didn't beat up the bad guys in public, though I'm sure He easily could have. What I do know is, He fought the schemes of the devil every day with the overwhelming, inexplicable love of God. Doesn't this sound like the kind of superhero you'd want to get to know, take out of the box, and play with?

Jesus doesn't just want us to enjoy Him. He invites all of us to train and become superheroes also. Jesus desires for people of all ages to take up the charge to do what He did and more.

When I was a young boy, I decided to tell Jesus I

wanted to spend the rest of my life learning to be a hero, just like Him. I told Him I wanted to know how to instil the fear of God into the most evil enemies. I asked Him to prepare me to respond to the tangible needs of others.

God gave me a tutorial and a master-plan called the Bible in which I could learn the best-kept hero secrets. When He left earth, Jesus gave us an incredible suit of armour called the Armour of God.

This hero sent us an incredible helper as well; one far more amazing than a goofy gymnast sidekick named Robin, who lost his parents in a freak carnival high-ropes accident. Jesus sent us one of the best sidekicks in history. This hero from Nazareth sent us one of his closest companions: The Holy Spirit. He knows all of my thoughts, motives, and goals for fighting corruption and evil. He's the guy who carries the real firepower when it comes to healing, knowledge, and destiny. When there's something I can't quite figure out on my own, I let this Spirit's superhuman powers override my weakness. We've been through all kinds of crazy capers together.

Doesn't this sound too good to be true? How can an average person suit up and take on the gangsters of our cities with a spiritual cape and cowl? We need to muster up the courage and childlike faith it takes to accept this call for our lives. One of the first steps is believing that God has called you to more than an average, boring life. We must draw close to Jesus, and take His leading and guidance in pursuing our hero destinies.

There are heroes all around us who we can learn from and grow to become like. Some of them attend our local churches, others own businesses, and others you might find serving at a homeless shelter, or are planning a missional trip to a third world country. These heroes often need help on their capers and quests. Why not take a risk and help them tackle a need in the city? If you don't have a dream yet for your own life, find someone who does and help them fight for theirs!

We might find our own heroic passions and grow in our spiritual abilities along the way too. We won't all look or act like Batman. Even though we are all members of the same superhero family, there is a vast spectrum of abilities and heroic endeavours for us to initiate.

It doesn't matter how old you are; all that matters is how bold you are.

This is a simple choice we must make each day because we don't arrive on this earth a hero. Heroism has to be drawn out of us through experiences, heartache, courage, and the continual fight to keep living until we are released to our destinies.

I hear a lot of tragic stories about kids, and adults too, who choose to end their lives before their lives ever really get started. There is a vicious, lawless super villain roaming around our city streets. This villain seeks to cut short the lives of any unsuspecting humans, who will listen to his cunning stories and disgusting deceit. This archenemy of Jesus and humanity is called Satan, and he can take many forms in our lives. Like the Joker, he wants to watch the entire world burn. His chief aim is to see God's creation in ruin, turmoil, and distress.

Before Jesus flew out of Earth to go back to his hero-cave in heaven, He left us with a call to kick the enemy's butt. He handed his power and authority over to a group of young adults He called his disciples. Jesus charged them to turn the entire world upside down for His glory, and to stomp the devil and his armies underneath their feet.

For the past two thousand years, God's army has been in battle, taking back ground from the enemy. Real people, like you and me, have been putting on their spiritual capes and body armour and facing up to the greatest evils here on Earth.

Jesus never promised us the hero's life would be easy. He promised us it would be a fight. Some of us would get bruised, beat up, and scarred along the way. But in the end, it would all be worth it.

You were called to be a superhero. Look at yourself in the mirror and own it until you believe it. Imagine your eight-year-old self declaring this, decked out in your favourite halloween costume. You were never meant merely to play with action figures while growing up, and to fantasize about imaginary victories in your imagination. You were born for your very own triumphs over evil in your lifetime.

The Bible says how God has planned amazing adventures for all to participate in; He's prepared good works for us to do. If you're feeling bored in this life, chances are, no one's told you that you're a superhero. Chances are, you are still standing in the toy store aisle, staring at Jesus on the shelf.

He is waiting for you to reach out and take hold of Him. He has called you to take Him out of the packaging, out of the religious boxes which we too often put Him into, and see who He really is, and what He has called us to become. Jesus promised us all He will be with us along the way. Jesus is calling you to a life of risk, a life of adventure, maybe even a life of danger.

This is the kind of superhero I want to take out of the box and play with.

FIVE

A Field Trip
to The Dentist

*I used to be addicted to candy,
but now I'm addicted to hope.*

I was laid out on their torture-table like a fattened calf on the chopping block. "Please pass me the syringe," the dentist starkly told the assistant.

I felt my mother rubbing my left foot: her attempt to distract me from a foot-long needle colliding with my jawbone. As the sedatives and anesthesia kicked in, all I could feel was the vibrating sensation of grinding, poking, prodding, and the misting of cold water on my face. Little did I know, they were grinding one of my molars down to a powder. The vivid depictions of oral surgery may be enough to make little children scream, but for me, it was just another all too frequent 'field trip' to the dentist.

Since I was homeschooled until I reached Junior High, I had the opportunity to indulge in many epic daytime outings. Going to the dentist was not one of them. My mother never seemed to care if I was horribly sick, or preoccupied with my latest third-grade business venture. She never let me miss a dental appointment.

She always attempted to ease my nerves with the

excuse, "Your father pays good money for these proce-dures, and we wouldn't want to cancel last-minute. I'm sure you'll feel fine once we get there."

"Yeah, I'll feel better after I pass out from the pain and shock of pulled teeth and blood splatters on the walls and ceiling," I retorted. Yes, I have a vivid imagination.

To say I didn't have the best teeth growing up would be an understatement. I vaguely remember my first trip to the dental office with my mother. The dentist literally swore when he took his first glance into my mouth. Maybe this gives you an idea of how I took care of my teeth—or didn't.

I had a love-hate relationship with my hygienist too. She would ask me if I'd been flossing regularly. I would quickly change the subject to the latest episode of Even Stevens and ask her whether she had seen it recent-ly? I figured I wouldn't be inherently lying if we focused her attention on more important matters.

After a few moments of banter, she would tilt and lower the chair backward, and point the ridiculously bright light directly at my retinas. If the half-hour gum scraping and tooth grinding session didn't kill you, the ultraviolet rays from the fluorescent lights would.

I wish I could say teeth cleaning was the pinnacle of pain and suffering for me when going to the dentist. But this was only scraping the tip of the iceberg, or the tip of the gum line. Depends on how you choose to look at it.

When I was about seven years old, I was watching The Indian In the Cupboard with my father one Friday evening. I chowed down on some lukewarm pizza when I felt a funny lump in my mouth. I didn't think it was a new tooth coming in, because it bulged on my gums, beside my teeth. I wandered into the bathroom to more closely observe this strange discovery in the mirror. There certainly was something unusual about this lump. The next day, guess where I wound up?

As much as I hated all things dental, I got along with my new dentist, Dr. Breault, fairly well. His warm demeanour and calming presence always reassured me, as painful as the procedures could be, I was still going to be okay.

My mouth had a lump on account of an abscess. The dentist had to pull my tooth to get rid of the lump. Having teeth pulled is not a fun experience.

So why all of these teeth problems? Well, more than a chapter about hating dentist visits, this is the harsh, gritty confession of an elementary kid with a violent addiction. One that tore my life apart at the very core. I would steal and lie to get my next fix.

My drug of choice was candy. I was a heavy user ever since I can remember. I would spend hours daydreaming about my next sugar high. It all started back at church in the early 90s. I was only three or four years old at the time.

I was too young to go to Sunday School, so my parents kept me with them in the services. Outside the auditorium, in the main foyer, stood a shiny, glass and silver candy machine propped up next to the coffee bar. In return for the spin-dial transaction, you got a fistful of candies. If you happened to be as short and small as I was, it delivered a whole armful of sweets.

My parents would search for me during the worship services, after I sneakily rolled under several rows of pews and peeled out the back of the room. I had acquired several quarters from the change jar in my father's top drawer, as well as a couple of coins from my monthly allowance. I began to salivate as I dropped my first quarter into the slot and heard the clunk sound. It resembled the ringing of a dinner bell, like the case of Pavlov's dog, except in this instance, I was the canine.

I slowly twisted the dial with both of my trembling hands. The grind of the gears spinning and opening sounded like a pinball machine. Then, time for the payoff. As soon as the rotation of the dial came to a sudden stop, I heard a tiny clicking sound. Suddenly, a waterfall of jelly beans of all shapes and colours spilled into my waiting palms. They poured out with such momentum and force that I could only catch half of them. The other half plummeted onto the carpeted floor. I would cautiously glance around the room to see if my parents were looking for me. I then proceeded to shove the sweets into my shallow pockets, handful by handful.

Over time, I slowly grew out of this life-threatening candy addiction, though I've had a half dozen relapses along the way.

There's no minimum age for when you're called an addict. We seem to pin adults with this label, but I feel people of all ages can relate to this. Addiction is everyone's story in some capacity. At some point, we've all tried to fill a God-sized hole with a gummy-bear solution. I've seen these patterns play out in my life in other areas over the years. After candy, I had an unhealthy addiction to social media. I hate to say that it still has been a problem for me at times. As we get older, we tend to cover up the pain of our childhoods with much more secretive and damaging quick-fixes than a candy habit.

Addiction can take many forms, but the issues which lie underneath the surface can be the most damaging. The sort of addictions I'm talking about are not the kind of stuff you get put in jail for or hear about on the news. These sorts of cravings are more sneaky and more damaging to the our inner child's soul. The drugs I've used were things like lying, cheating, lust, name-calling, fakery, as well as manipulating others in an attempt to get my way. These addictive traits and habits are common in our present world. These bad habits can destroy relationships, cripple our self-esteem, and leave our childlike wonder and hopes in utter distress and ruin.

I know a lot of people struggle with real drug addictions too, and by no means do I want to downplay the seriousness of this problem. I've walked through the streets of East Hastings in downtown Vancouver.

As I surveyed those city streets, I would wonder to myself how people end up being ensnared in such a troubling lifestyle. It's crazy to think those were the type of people Jesus chose to hang out with; the prostitutes, the pimps, the vandals, the drug dealers, and the vagrants. Maybe He was so drawn to these people because they all knew they had this God-sized cavity which needed filling. They were using what was in front of them in an attempt to patch up these holes. These broken, hurting people resembled young children, chowing down on handfuls of candy in the church foyer. These outcasts cared more about the feeling they would receive from their drug of choice than the opinions of others. They were passionate people, waiting for a better fix or a better high. They were calling out for a permanent high with no negative side effects or withdrawal symptoms.

When we find ourselves at the bottom of the barrel, the bottom rung of the ladder, we have nowhere to go but up. This is where Jesus seems to swoop in and meet with beautiful, broken people. It's where He often showed up for me.

A passionate, creative songwriter and king from the Bible named David once said how when we are broken down, and at the end of ourselves, we'll find God right there. I used to think I would only find God at the church services, somewhere between the opening greetings and the closing prayers. I never guessed I would find Jesus in the eyes of my dentist, as I sat thrashing in pain.

Jesus isn't freaked out about the state of our lives, or the state of our mouths, either. He is far more concerned about the position of our hearts. If I've learned anything from following Jesus, it's how He's the Great Physician, or the Great Dentist, you could say.

We've all walked into His dental office, struggling with swollen gums, spiritual cavities, and crooked smiles. We too often hate lying down on the reclining chair. But He doesn't judge us when He peers into the mouth of our lives. Jesus is completely engaged in the renovation process. The Great Dentist looks less at our failures and setbacks than you would think. In fact, He sees our beautiful smile taking shape before we can imagine our smiles or lives ever getting better.

Jesus knows even though we've lost all of our baby teeth, we haven't lost all of our childlike heart. I used to think I was disqualified from having a bright smile again, like I had when I was a kid. The cavities and evidence of pain, addiction, and decay plagued my heart and mind, and I could find no hope in sight. We need not run from the pain of this renovation process, either. Choosing to embrace a little bit of pain along the way will help us heal better in the end.

We need to muster up the courage to imagine us climbing onto the dental chair and let Jesus examine our lives. When Jesus peers with His light and mirror into the open mouth of our lives, He doesn't see a bunch of crowded, cavity-stricken teeth. He sees something beautiful taking shape inside of us. Jesus knows if a few teeth have to be pulled along the way, He's going to make it worth our while, because giving us a beautiful smile is one of His best practices.

SIX

Tree Forts & Bad Apples

I used to dig traps for my enemies, but Jesus
taught me to build bridges instead.

My childhood yard backed onto a beautiful ravine full of trees. I'm sure my parents decided to purchase that particular property because of the giant yard. The forest behind our place was a free form of daycare for us kids. My mom knew I would never wander too far off when a playground to outmatch all other playgrounds stood right behind our backyard.

A large ravine backed directly onto my yard, as well as every other backyard on our crescent, separating the houses from the main roadway behind them. It was public land which few people cared to walk in, but in my mind, it was Justin's Wonderland.

The summer I was eight years old, I climbed trees and played for hours on end in the spectacular ravine. Whenever I grew hungry, I would sneakily climb over our neighbour's fence and pick armfuls of crabapples in his yard. If you ate them earlier on in the season as I did, they packed quite the sour punch. These apples were only this tasty and crisp for about three weeks of the year, so I made sure to gorge myself any chance I got. My elderly neighbour, Mr. Anderson, didn't pay too much attention to me when I would climb his tree to consume bushels of apples. I never saw him pick the apples either, so I figured they would go to waste if I didn't help myself to them, and I was doing Mr. Anderson a favour. My poor, elderly neighbour was reaching the end of his life. Eventually, he passed on, and the house went up for sale. A new neighbour moved in a few weeks later. His name was Glen, and he was planning to build a garage beside his house. I remember examining the yard and deciding a garage wouldn't matter to me, because the awesome apple tree stood fairly far back in the yard. But when the workers came out and began framing the garage, my worst nightmare unfolded. Glen had decided to build his garage twice as deep as a normal one. He wanted to park two vehicles inside, one behind the other. My crabapple days were over.

I stared dismally over the fence as the workers took their chainsaws to the tree, branch by branch, limb by limb. The apples began to fall, and the tree seemed to squeal in desperation as my hopes and dreams of my next sour fix crashed to the ground. The only sour feeling I was going to have in my stomach from now on was the guttural sensation of pure hatred toward my new arch nemesis of a neighbour. If he was trying to make enemies before he had made friends, he was doing a pretty good job of it.

I sank into a deep depression after this sour catastrophe. My father sympathized with me in my desperate state and often tried to take my mind off of my frustrations with Glen. We went to the local greenhouse, and I picked out a small crabapple tree to plant in our yard. This infantile excuse for a tree could never replace the tree of life next door. This tree didn't even have any apples on it!

One afternoon soon after this, my father brought home a truckload of two-by-four boards from his work. He dumped the load of lumber in our backyard on the grass. I forgot the apple tree and its pathetic replacement immediately. All I could think about was the colossal tree fort I was going to build with my friends that summer in the ravine behind my house. I immediately phoned up my skateboarder pal, Derek, from down the street and explained my epic construction plans to him. He cleared his schedule at once and brought his older cousin along to help, too.

We didn't have to cut any of the boards to make them any shorter, because they were all roughly two feet long. All we were missing were nails, so we smashed open our piggy banks, filled our pockets with coins, and raced down to the local hardware store.

I had a pretty good idea of the sort of tree fort we were going to build; but rather than think too hard about the details, we went straight to work without any formal planning. I don't know how many twelve to fifteen-hour days we poured into this project, but we spent a great deal of time and effort on it.

Time flew by as we made progress on our towering tree fort in the ravine. We decided to make the main floor of the fort high above our heads, six feet up into the group of trees. We found mismatched and oddly- shaped slabs of particleboard and plywood to hammer down along the surface of the main floor. This main landing was larger than your average bedroom and spanned out with a bridge leading to several other trees. We built a small lookout tower higher up in the main tree. From the tower, we were high enough to spy on Glen's backyard.

My young building crew stood in awe, viewing our amazing creation. I imagined how God felt after He created our world, on the seventh day, when He finally had time to sit back and gaze at His creation and say, "Man, this thing is good." We had built something remarkable together. The fort wasn't only a hideout for kids our age, or a pile of wood stuck to a couple of trees. This creation was our sanctuary, our escape, our haven where we would be free to dream big and create any story we wanted to tell.

Sunday morning soon arrived, and my parents had to coax me down from the fort to get me to church. As the pastor preached his sermon, I visualized my friends and me preparing the fort for an enemy invasion, armed with wooden swords, pocket knives, and childlike excitement.

Our family arrived home from church early in the afternoon, and I was excited to check on my fort. As I stepped out of the car, a lightning bolt of tension shocked me to the core. The first thing I heard was a commotion coming from the ravine. Sounds of boards falling, crowbars slamming, and saws cutting echoed through the yard. My worst fears billowed up in my chest as I raced my way into the ravine.

My neighbour Glen, and his girlfriend, had taken it upon themselves to dismantle my epic tree fort completely. Boards and pieces of plywood were strewn all over the ground. The demolition squad had been working for a while, and I had arrived too late to save anything.

Tears filled my eyes as I bolted back to my house and screamed the news to my father. I was desperate, angry, and shattered on the inside. I didn't deserve such a harsh blow to my childlike heart.

I heard from the grapevine that they tore the fort down because it was an eyesore from their yard. What may not have seemed like a big deal to my neighbours was a ridiculously big deal to me.

My childlike mind full of hope and passionate creativity took a rocky detour into valleys of bitterness, anger, and resentment. My inner child's heart was all chewed up and broken.

Living next door to your mortal enemy isn't easy. I struggled for a few days conspiring how and when I would retaliate against this unspeakable crime.

I dug a large hole a week later. Instead of digging to China, I drilled a hole deep into my heart. I caved my way into a tunnel where nobody would be able to hurt me again. I dug a physical hole in the ravine too, hoping my neighbours would fall into it and be trapped there forever. I ingeniously placed the hole a few yards from my neighbour's back gate.

After hours of digging, my hole became deep enough to snare any unsuspecting victims who wandered by, or so I thought. By my estimations, the hole was at least four feet deep. But to a youngster like me, it felt like a mile! I figured it would be deep enough for my mean neighbour Glen to fall into. I planned to cover the hole with light branches, brush, and leaves, to camouflage my devious trap. When my neighbour wandered into the ravine for a stroll, he would succumb to my sly entrapment.

The following days flew by in anticipation, and yet again, I made an upsetting discovery. Glen had been one step ahead of me. He had filled in my enormous hole with compost! My plan to snare my neighbour fell through on me instead. I felt like I was at the bottom of the dark hole, buried in a mess of apple cores, rotten tomatoes, and egg shells.

Jesus promised us we would all experience major hangups and disappointments in our lifetimes, as I experienced back then. He mentioned how we would meet a few bad apples and mean characters along the way, too. Sometimes these mean people would even be our next-door neighbours! The real test is how we choose to respond to those who've wronged us. Jesus said it's never our job to shovel up revenge on our neighbours or our enemies. More often than not, revenge ends up backfiring on us. It robs us of our childlike innocence. It cripples our wonder and our inner child's pure intentions. Jesus calls us to love those who have wronged us and to practice forgiveness, even when it hurts.

Forgiveness is the one thing nobody deserves, but everyone desperately needs.

Forgiveness is challenging, especially when someone has hugely wronged us. We might find it easier to forgive people we like, but it's an entirely different story to forgive people we don't call our friends. True forgiveness is climbing out of the smelly pit of resentment in which we can so easily become trapped in. It can take a long time to climb out of this hole, especially if we continue digging deeper into unforgiveness with our shovels. Jesus promises us forgiving others is worth it in the end, because holding a grudge ends up hurting us and keeping us enslaved to our anger.

I chose to forgive my neighbour Glen for his actions toward me because I know Jesus has forgiven me for my wrongdoings. Unfortunately, it took a decade to forgive my mean neighbour. I thought things would get easier with time, but things just got messier. The longer I sat at the bottom of that hole of unforgiveness, the more smelly compost piled on top of me. My grudge against Glen was a festering open wound inside my chest that needed healing. The darkness of this hole I lived in slowly suffocated my childlike wonder until I began to forget all about the child-like hopes and dreams God once placed inside of me.

Jesus doesn't want our lives left in shambles like a torn down tree fort from our past. It isn't part of His plan to see us covered in compost, sitting at the bottom of a smelly, bitter predicament either.

Maybe you've had your childlike fort of dreams come crashing down in front of you as I did. You have felt like there's no possible chance these dreams could ever get put back together again. Jesus wants us all to realize that the painful memories don't have to define who we are. He is the Master Builder of our lives, waiting for us to embark on His wonderful blueprints.

Fixes don't always happen so easily. We may spend much of our lives in repair: picking up the plywood, the broken two-by-fours, the nails, and the scraps of our lives. Healing our hearts and our hopes take time, even if we've done our part of forgiving others. We rarely forget the actions of those who have seriously wronged us. We need to carefully plant seeds of hope in the soil of our lives, in place of where our seeds of bitterness and unforgiveness once took root. With courage, we will pick up what remains of our dreams and build something beautiful with the worn and broken pieces of lumber.

God's plan for us is to build a childlike masterpiece with our lives, like the Brooklyn Bridge, or the Great Wall of China. He desires we begin this masterpiece by building a pathway of love which reaches out to our enemy's yard with love and forgiveness.

Let's start to pick up the broken down tree forts and apple trees of our lives, and build a bridge called forgiveness instead. The firm foundation of this bridge is choosing to pray for those who have wronged us. This bridge will tower high over our disappointments and our bitterness, and span a pathway of forgiveness to even our worst enemies. This beautiful structure will create a solid foundation for new adventures, new dreams, and new incredible stories to share.

I asked my neighbour Glen recently if he remembers tearing down my tree fort. He quickly stated that he didn't recall the event. I don't know if I believe him or not, but I sure do forgive him.

SEVEN

Karate Kiddo

I used to pick fights with the devil,
but now I know Jesus has won the war.

Throwing the first punch at your opponent's chest is exhilarating. I loved the thrill of grabbing the cuffs of my opponent's outfit, pivoting my foot behind his shin, and slamming him down onto a rubber mat. I can recall a few occasions where I walked into the change room after a Karate training session with a shiner the size of Texas above my right cheek. I knew every battle wound was inching me ever closer to Bruce Lee's black belt stardom status.

If parents ever plotted ways to use up their children's excessive energy, weekly activities like Karate were their secret weapon. I think every kid should learn self-respect and self-discipline at a young age. There's also a lot of value in a seven-year-old knowing how to effortlessly pulverize a burglar, school bully, or a back alley attacker. Our Sensei would often remind us how karate was a lifestyle of honour, courage, and a higher standard of excellence.

I was a rather tiny kid at the age of six, when I took up this wonderful martial art. In fact, I didn't grow an awful lot, vertically or horizontally, throughout my child-hood karate career. I heard my friends and their parents talk about the idea of a growth spurt. My friends seemed to hit their growth spurts in a flash, sort of like a hun-dred-yard sprint. Mine resembled a senior citizen fun run with free donuts and coffee.

Bystanders and other parents may have wondered if I had an eating disorder, or if my parents couldn't afford to feed me cheeseburgers and spaghetti. But that wasn't the case at all. My parents fed me heaps of food! A fast metabolism must have been in my genes. I would often find myself comparing my height to guys like young King David or Zacchaeus from the Bible. They lacked the whole adolescent-growth-spurt phase too. I'm sure they had to learn to throw a harder punch in their own karate classes because of it.

Since I was homeschooled until Junior High, Karate class was a great place for me to make friends. It's cool to be able to fight people you really like and walk away smiling at the end of the sparring match. As I progressed through my colourful belt years, from white to yellow, then green to blue and so on, my rank, skill level, and passion quickly grew. But my height and weight sure didn't.

I found myself attending the young adult Saturday morning sessions at the age of ten. Everyone else in the class was taller than me, and I tried my best to pretend it didn't bother me, but deep down inside it did. I would spar with an older friend of mine named Matthew, who was about two feet taller than I was, and he must have weighed nearly two hundred pounds. Matt could probably have eaten my weight in bacon for a light protein breakfast. He was a good friend, but he was a little bit on the clumsy side.

Our class instructor would blow the whistle to announce the beginning of the fight. We would pivot our feet and shift our weight in quick and calculated rhythms, attempting to predict the opponent's first strike. In the game of sparring, you need three direct hits to win the match. One of the rules is you cannot make contact with your opponent's head, or you get a penalty and a warning. After a few minutes, I swiftly landed a sweet left jab to Matthew's exposed ribcage and gained a point. Then suddenly, out of nowhere, his left fist came hurtling toward my head. I heard a sudden, loud SMACK as his black foam glove made contact with my unsuspecting face. Sensei blew the warning whistle at us, reminding Matt how head-shots were not permitted. He then nodded at me to ensure I was feeling okay from the jarring impact.

I tried to take it like a ninja, nodding back and welcoming another round with a "bring it on, chum" sort of demeanour.

Another round flew by. Matt landed two good blows, and I returned the favour with a smooth, round-house kick. We were two for two. Watching this giant junior high kid take on my scrawny younger self, resembled watching David daringly battle Goliath. My friend was throwing his punches straight down at a very bizarre, awkward angle.

The sparring match heated up as time went on, both of us desperate to land the final victory blow. Then, like a bad dream, Matt must have forgotten about his downward angle, and his fist slammed into my face. I bounced back from the shock of the impact and shook out my head, attempting to gather my brain marbles.

Sensei asked if I was okay. I nodded my head. He

quickly blew his whistle three times and pulled up my right hand in a sign of victory. Matt had been disqualified for his headshot, and I was given the final, winning point.

I tried to fight back the tears which slowly welled up in my eyes. I had never felt so embarrassed in my whole life! I knew Matt hadn't intended to hit me in the head, and thanks to the rubber padding, I wasn't in too much pain, but what hurt the most was that I hadn't won the match on my own merits. A lie formed in my heart, whispering that I would always be small, and I should give up on the whole karate thing altogether.

I had accomplished much during my karate days and was only two stripes and a tests away from receiving my junior black belt. Most teenagers don't earn this belt until sometime after middle school. I was boldly doing my best to perform my karate craft with excellence and determination, and all the while my growth spurt was at a standstill. I felt completely embarrassed and ashamed of my appearance. I didn't want to become the laughing stock of the class or a human Whack-a-Mole, so I decided to drop karate altogether and bow out of the experience.

After quitting karate, a blur of emotions whirled in my mind. I desperately wanted to stay at the club, but I knew if I did, I would have those same thoughts of discouragement, self-hatred, and constant comparisons to others. I recall angrily praying to God at night in my room, begging Him to help me grow even an inch or two taller, or for my tiny hands to grow bigger before I woke up the next morning. My tears and pleas for help seemed to amount to nothing.

My parents decided to enrol me in public education for middle school. I was really good at making new friends there, and apparently, there were a couple of rumours going around about me and my karate skills.

I would hear kids talking about me behind my back, saying how I killed a guy once, or how the bullies should stay away from me because I had been training with ninjas in Japan. All I needed to preserve my minuscule seventh-grade self from bodily harm was a hint of gossip and a larger-than-life rumour which I never denied.

Whatever I lacked in height and body mass, I made up for in mystery and intrigue. I loved playing the part of this dangerous rebel. A few of my hulky friends would fill me in on the details of any upcoming fights at school. They asked for my expert advice, if the matchups were fair, and if I had any recommendations for their contending fighter. I often deterred the use of weapons, unless they came in the form of rubber padding or nerf bullets.

I played my tough-guy role whenever I lacked self-confidence and went along with their little games and assumptions. It's like the other kids thought I could defeat the entire boy's gym class with a twelve-inch ruler and some dental floss. These antics went on for quite some time, and I kept playing this fictitious character for weeks on end.

This whole charade eventually began to wear down my childlike spirit. I felt so empty on the inside, because I wasn't allowing others to get to know the real me. In fact, I wasn't quite sure who the real me was anymore. I had become something I hated. I wanted to be loved by real friends, and I desperately wanted the strength to love myself.

I wish I could tell you it's easy to love yourself, especially when you're twelve and only weigh seventy-two pounds. Loving yourself despite what you look like on the outside isn't always easy. Many of us attempt to "love" those around us, all the while neglecting to love ourselves. It's a form of false humility masquerading as love.

Jesus calls us to have a fresh childlike perspective for our lives. He would say to His disciples how we need to love our friends as we love ourselves. You see, love has to come from inside us, where we first love the person God created us to be. It is then a lot easier and real to extend our love to others.

Nobody has it easy today. I've learned how these struggles often begin in our teenage years. So many youths in schools today begin battling with eating disorders, identity issues, and self-harming thoughts and tendencies. The real enemy we need to pick a fight with is the crippling problem of comparison.

We are all guilty of wanting to be like somebody else at one time or another. Maybe it's your neighbour, a friend from work, or a celebrity on television. We strive to be more like others around us because we believe that we aren't good enough to be accepted or loved the way that we are. Deep down inside of us, a kid is crying in his bedroom, wishing others would love him for who he really is. Choosing to fall for the crutch of comparison sabotages our childlike wonder, our innocence and our reliance on God.

The process of self-love and respect is a slow and sometimes painful road, especially when the damages of comparison have crippled our inner child for years. A good friend of mine, who is a successful recording artist, once told me he was tired of seeking validation from others and trying to be somebody he wasn't ever made to be. He recently decided to make a startling and tough career change from secular music to Christian music. He always wanted his music and talent to glorify God. He couldn't bear the thought of thousands of screaming fans worshipping him on stage, when all the while, he felt he should be pointing their praises to God.

He decided to take a leap of childlike faith by risking his established reputation and switching gears in his music career path. We both came to the conclusion that people are going to love us or hate us, regardless of whether we are pretending or being real. So we might as well be real and receive genuine love in return. Doctor Seuss emphatically communicates this same sentiment, "Why fit in when you were born to stand out?"

A prophet from the Bible named Jeremiah stated how God knew us before He formed us in our mother's wombs. Before we were born, God set us apart. We are His favourite part of creation, and He can't stop bragging about us to His friends. We are God's greatest dream come true. He's constantly smiling down from heaven upon us. God even states how we are fearfully and wonderfully made. He knows how many hairs are on our heads, when we can barely count our blessings.

I always wondered what the whole "fearfully" part meant. Does this mean God is scared He made us? I don't think so. I think it means the spiritual enemies of God, and even the other parts of creation, stand in wonder and awe at the sight of us. We are made in the likeness and image of God, our creator. Our enemy, the devil, hates us for strutting our God-given stuff around like red carpet celebrities. No matter how old you are or how you feel about yourself, you are seriously, totally, hot stuff. It's time to stand in awe and childlike wonder again the next time we look at selves in the mirror. We can rest assured that God doesn't make mistakes in His design of us. He only knows how to create masterpieces.

I'm pleased to say I finally hit my growth spurt a year or two after graduating high school. Just in time for all of the cute girls to never see me in my adult swagger. I'm able to chuckle about it now, but not all of the pain of those childhood lies and troubling feelings easily goes away. Jesus is like my skilled karate instructor. He gives us the tools necessary to defend ourselves when our identities are under attack. He's taught me lately to pick a fight against the spiritual school bullies that hurt and devalue our childlike spirits. These bullies are comparison, shame, guilt, and false identities.

The Bible says that our battle isn't against flesh and blood, but against spiritual forces in the unseen realm. These sneaky, spiritual bullies attack the core of who God has made us to be. These bullies throw verbal punches and uppercut lies like "you're ugly," "you're useless," and "you're not good enough," all day long.

Sooner or later, we start believing these false notions, and they become who we are on the inside.

The devil pushes us around in the hallways of our lives when we aren't strong enough to stand up for ourselves. Thankfully, Jesus has our backs in this fight when we feel abandoned, lost, and alone. Only He can teach us how to readily defend ourselves against the devil. The key to these sparring matches with the enemy is to keep your chin up and keep your head in the game. The enemy plans to see us give up before we hit our spiritual growth spurts in this life. I already know what giving up on something important to me feels like. Now I want to see when I don't give up!

I've had my fair share of cheap shots from the devil in my lifetime. It's in those moments, I must look to God and ask Him for help, to remind me who I really am, and who He's called me to be.

Jesus teaches His friends how training in righteousness is the best kind of training. It's the kind of workout which deals a deadly blow to false identity and comparison. The kind of self-defence training I'm talking about offers real hope to those of us living in this crazy, messed up, adult world.

We must utilize a childlike faith to clothe ourselves in the full armour of God. Our master teacher has given us a giant, bully-slaying, ninja sword called the Bible, which cuts down the lies and attacks of the enemy, if we choose to wield it and swing into action. We must make a daily effort to train with this Sword of the Spirit and to digest the truths that it holds about who God created us to be. These truths can be found in every page of the scriptures. We must pray for the childlike curiosity to search out these truths and allow them to penetrate our souls to the core.

Our karate King Jesus has given us a hefty shield called faith. It protects us against the darts and lies of the enemy. This childlike faith believes that God is bigger and stronger than any circumstances or obstacles we may face. This faith stands strong in trials and believes that when God stands for us, no one can stand against us. It's the kind of faith that gives children the strength to slay giants, and elderly men the courage to lead nations. Jesus wants to remind us how He is able to sympathize with our weaknesses and gives us His strength and power in those challenging times. Jesus offers us our own spiritual black belt too. It's a reward for running a good race and fighting a good fight in this lifetime. This black belt is a reminder that Jesus has already defeated our enemies on our behalf. We no longer need to fight out of a place of victimhood, but we can fight out of a place of victory instead.

We must consciously commit to putting on the full armour of God each day. It's our safeguard against the enemy's tactics and assaults. When Jesus leans down and ties the karate belt of truth around the waist of our lives, He peacefully says, "You are fearfully and wonderfully made. You were born for this. You are mine. Now go kick some butt!"

EIGHT

The Pet Detective

*I used to think this cage didn't have an exit,
but now I know Jesus is the door.*

My family didn't want to own a dog in my younger years, because raising me was all the work my parents could handle. I got my first pet at the age of nine when my friend Derek brought some interesting critters over; strange, twig-like insects called walking sticks. These peculiar creatures blended in perfectly with their surroundings, looking exactly like their name. I begged my parents to let me have my own walking sticks. They didn't have to think hard about it before agreeing to my pleas, and Derek was happy to give me a couple of his tiny bug friends.

I gathered some leaves, stones, and grass for the critters and placed them in an old fish tank. Derek had fun showing off his bugs at school and around the neighbourhood. I showed mine to my sister because I was still home-schooled. A few days passed before my father approached me with a startling discovery. These insects were banned in our town. Apparently, they would multiply like rabbits and start taking over green, grassy areas. My father said a bylaw report stated that we must exterminate any walking sticks, or pay a fine for failure to do so. My poor walking sticks said goodbye to me in a blaze of glory in the backyard fire pit, and my short-lived career as a pet owner was over.

Thankfully, I had numerous other pastimes to fill my days, and Saturday morning cartoons and my favorite show, Mr. Dressup, soon replaced the memory of my unfortunate critters.

Welcome to my childhood of whimsy. Homeschooling granted me a beautiful start on my childlike, wide-eyed dreams at a young age. While my friends were stuck in structured rows, writing tests, I was blazing my own trails. A world of wonder and adventure was aching to bounce out of my chest every chance it got.

I saw a desperate need for a suburban dog wrangler in my neighbourhood, so I jumped into action. If anyone saw a stray dog, the neighbours knew who to call. I had my business cards fresh off the printing press. I even used an actual typewriter to make them. The business cards read "Encyclopedia Wiesinger - Pet Detective." It had a nice ring to it.

One of my closest neighbours had a beautiful Norwegian Elkhound named Jacob. I often took Jake for walks during the day when his owner, Don, was away at work. Jake and I would stroll through the neighbourhood for hours together. I would ask him what it's like to be a dog, and if it's weird to have to poop in front of his family and friends. I would ask Jacob what he hoped to become in his lifetime. I wasn't looking for an audible answer, of course, because he was a dog! I was looking for a true friend, and this is exactly what Jake was to me.

One fateful afternoon, I was flying down Gilmore Crescent on my skateboard, passing Jake's home, when I heard frantic barking. I knew something was wrong, because this was a whole new level of barking for Jake. I jumped off my skateboard and approached the backyard for a better look. I was shocked to discover a second dog inside Jake's kennel: a giant, mean-looking Doberman-Hound cross. This discovery alarmed me because the exterior fence that surrounded Jake's yard was nearly ten feet tall. Jake and the mystery dog were locked inside his dog run within the yard. I wondered how this large dog was able to jump so high. He must have been quite the determined animal to attempt such a daring feat. This second dog lurking in Jake's kennel was totally unfamiliar to me. Judging by Jake's desperate demeanour, he was unsure about this dog, too. I knew that this animal wasn't supposed to be in there, and he was up to no good.

Jake didn't need better locks on his kennel. He didn't need sharper teeth or a larger overbite. What Jake needed was a true friend to rescue him. I couldn't leave my favourite canine in the world stuck with a potentially mean bully as an unwelcome guest.

I devised a plan of attack as I inched closer to Jake's kennel. My gut was telling me not to touch the big, mean-looking dog. Somehow, I needed to help Jake escape and leave the mangy beast in the prison where he belonged.

I quickly glanced around the backyard for anything that could help with my unfolding plan. I discovered a bag of dog treats left outside by the back door. I quickly created a diversion by throwing some of the goodies toward the back of Jake's long kennel. Once the burly dog caught the smell of the taunting snacks, he charged the length of the enclosure to claim them. I nervously watched as the ogre-like beast bent his snout down to devour these tasty treats. Then I sprinted around to the other side of the kennel and opened the latch to let Jake out. After Jake was safely behind me, I shut the kennel gate to trap this over-sized menace.

The mean-looking dog turned around and stared at us with desperation and confusion in his eyes. I could envision his looming prison sentence at the local pound dawning on his mangy conscience. I had clearly beaten this mutt at his own game. Jacob, my best canine friend in the world, was safe by my side.

I've never experienced a real-life home invasion like Jake did that day, but I've received surprise visits from unwelcome people on occasion. One of these unwanted guests was my so-called friend who showed me pornography for the first time when I was nine. I vividly remember another time when this same neighbour sexually abused me. He and his brother cornered me in his yard, and he taunted me while dropping his trousers in front of me. I was utterly horrified. I ran home crying, but those unwelcome guests called shame and pornography tagged along with me, too. Shame barged its way into my childhood, slobbering over my childlike innocence, acting like he owned the place. Shame was like that mangy dog, peeing on the carpet in my room, chewing on my favourite shoes, and even stealing my dinner.

We can rarely tell these intruders to leave on our own strength. As far as we're concerned, our master is at work, and we have no idea how to open the gate of our hearts, even if we wanted to.

When we're locked in the same room together, these slimy, wanna-be roommates look a lot larger and tougher than us. When Shame barges its way into our lives, it puffs itself up and intimidates us if we let it hang around long enough. When we finally get to the point of crying out for help, we hope somebody brave is standing nearby listening.

I let the burden of my smelly roommates named Shame and Lust torment me for far too long. I didn't cry out for help until high school. Fortunately, my parents were present to hear my cries. I told them how I was struggling with pornography and needed a friend to help me wipe away my guilt and shame. Around the same time, I opened up to a trusted friend about the incident of childhood sexual abuse. For years, I had downplayed the incident, believing that it wasn't a big deal.

The enemy loves to lie to us that our childhood scars should be kept secret and aren't important. I found so much freedom in seeking help that day. A young boy had been trapped deep inside a dark prison of shame but was now free to breathe again. I was released, and my childlike wonder began to return.

In the Bible, a fellow named Paul talked a lot about exposing the darkness of our lives and letting the light of Christ pour out over our sin, shame, and regrets. He said those of us who were asleep in darkness needed the light of Christ to shine upon us and expose the hidden places in our lives. It's like we all need an awakening at one time or another where our childlike selves rise from their slumber.

Children are never meant to grow up at such a young age. Many of us are thrown into prison cells at an early age with a life sentence called a loss of innocence.

Maybe it's a moment of abuse which triggered this event, or a trauma which was too much for youngsters to bear. All of a sudden, we froze, forced to grow up and cover up this horrible memory. We buried the event to protect ourselves from the pain of facing up to the painful incidents. We chose to put on an adult-sized mask and use an adult-sized coping mechanism, which all too often takes the form of hidden sin.

If we keep living in avoidance and letting our past pains cripple us, we risk never living out our inner child's meaningful life in the first place.

The ugly lens of guilt, shame, and chaos paints and discolours a life intended for wonder, joy, and discovery. Sure we still went through the motions of life, but our true childlike self was held hostage on Skull Island. What we need the most is the courage to cry out for help, trusting that we have a friend and saviour nearby listening. Like Jake, we desperately need a true friend who is always there to cover us and protect us at a moment's notice.

I don't know what sort of thoughts and emotions were going through Jacob's head that afternoon, but I know he was calling for a friend to come and help.

Jesus has taught me a thing or two about showing love to others. I can never stop talking about Jesus because He's crazy about loving you and me. He's relentlessly pursuing us. Jesus explains that the best kind of love is to lay down your life for your friends. I bet Jesus was alluding to His victory on the cross, but I also know He was talking about us responding to this same call for our own lives.

We don't lay down our lives so others will like us more, or so they think we're the hero. We do it when nobody is watching, seeking a reward from our Heavenly

Master, rather than from a few neighbourhood friends. We don't have to die in a blaze of glory and bullets the next time our friends cry out for help. There's no need to Snapchat or Facebook live the entire event to ensure somebody is watching you save the day.

This call for brotherly love does mean we should act according to the measure of faith God has extended to us. And if we want to become more, and love more, we have to keep asking for longer walks around the block with Jesus, all the while continuing to listen to His promises spoken over us.

So many people around us are desperately calling out like my friend Jacob did, or like I did after the troubling encounters with my neighbour. Many desperate people feel like they're locked up in a dog pen with a slobbery, unwelcome guest. Intruders and enemies of God are jumping fences and causing trouble in the lives of those we love. Children who experience sexual harassment and abuse need friends and heroes like you and me to stick up for them in a moment's notice. We need to pray for the childlike ears to hear their cries in the city streets, in the playgrounds, and in their homes. We must posture ourselves to be good listeners so our friends can find comfort and courage to speak out about their past hurts. We need to do an extra lap or two around our neighbourhoods, with our skateboards in hand, so they know we're listening.

One thing I've learned from following Jesus is He is always only a whisper away. He's saved me from a few unwelcome guests in my lifetime, and the least I can do is return the favour to a few friends in need of a jailbreak.

NINE

Pot Shots & Dead Meat

I used to be scared of consequences,
but now I'm grateful for God's grace.

At the age of ten, I hadn't yet heard the blast and crackle of my father's Remington rifle, but I was anxious to feel the trembling aftershock of his gun.

I've been on some memorable hunting trips with my father; this first trip out with him was no exception. We arrived at his friend's acreage fairly late one afternoon in early November. My father and I planted ourselves on a small ridge which overlooked a vast clearing. This positioning gave us a strategic view across the main game trails. Before long, we heard a noise coming from a couple hundred yards away, inside the edge of the woods. My father nodded at me to put on my ear muffs. I obeyed and prepared for an epic show of heroic firepower. Bambi was in for a shock. I quietly observed my father as he rested his elbow on a conveniently-placed tree limb. He leaned part of his weight against the tree while planting his feet firmly in a battle stance. The tension rose as my father cocked his rifle. Before I could count to ten, I caught a direct visual of the blast of gunpowder and heard a giant bang ring out as the bullet zipped across the clearing toward the helpless deer. Immediately after the gun blast, my father stumbled to the ground, placing his hand across his face, as if in shock. A pool of blood slowly oozed from the bridge of his nose and started trickling down his right cheek onto the frosty ground.

My father didn't score his trophy buck that night, but he got a trophy scar and a bruise on his face, and I should have paid closer attention to proper gun safety. Unfortunately, the most memorable hunting adventure of my childhood took place in my own backyard a few weeks later.

Being handed your first BB gun as a kid is a surreal experience. It's a similar feeling to graduating college, getting your license, or going on your first date. You feel like the master of your domain: awarded a brand new, grown-up badge of honour, achieving a whole new level of cool.

My parents ordered me not to play with the new gun in the yard. They should have locked the weapon up in a vault. I discovered the poorly-hidden rifle in the basement, and I snuck it into the backyard one afternoon while my parents were out running errands. I was far too rambunctious to save this treasure for hunting trips with my father.

I didn't need Facebook or a Twitter feed to spread news virally in my tight-knit neighbourhood. I quickly made some overexcited phone calls to a few friends: Troy, the tall, lanky one who owned pretty much every single Pokemon card available, and Derek, the crazy and unpredictable skateboarder who was a few years older than me and attended a French immersion junior/senior high school. In mere minutes, my whole team of mighty men was on hand to bicker over who was going to fire the gun next, while we crept through the ravine near my house in hopes of slaying a stray lion, tiger, or bear.

Large game eluded us, however, and all we found were some over-pretentious squirrels and the odd magpie observing our inexperienced hunting techniques. My friends and I took potshots at anything in sight. We shot at trees, telephone posts, squirrels, and rocks.

The chances of a stray pellet hitting a car were astronomical because the main roadway passed only a hundred feet away from the ravine. My nerves snowballed as my friends grew more anxious to draw first blood with this shiny new instrument of destruction. I feared that my parents would soon find out that I was using the gun without their permission.

All of a sudden, my hyperactive friend, Derek, aimed the gun and shot at a magpie. Direct hit! The bird bounced off a few tree branches and plummeted to the ground with a terrifying kerplunk. 133

My heart thundered in my chest as I witnessed my first murder. I quickly calculated the best place to dig a hole, hide the body, and dump the evidence before the police came knocking. My friends and I had disobeyed my parents, and an innocent bird had paid the price of our folly. I was in big trouble. I grabbed the gun from Derek and told the boys that playtime was over. I slunk back to the house, hoping to put the gun away before my parents came home.

A few minutes later, before I returned upstairs, I heard violent yelling in the yard, and Troy frantically screaming my name. I dashed outside to see what the fuss was about. "Justin, Justin! You need to come out here now! Oh man, this is really, really bad."

Troy was short of breath, and his eyes were bugging out like he had seen someone get hit by a car. Or worse! "Justin, I'm sorry! I—we—we shouldn't have let him pick up the bird!" "Pick up the bird?" I asked, confused. "What are you talking about?"

Troy, trembling with fear, frantically unravelled the horrifying event. "Derek ran down to the street and threw the bird at a van!" My hands grew clammy. "The bird exploded!" Troy wailed. "There's blood and guts and feathers all over the windshield!"

My mouth flapped, but no sound came out.
"And Justin!" Troy was panting for breath. "The guys in the van are twelfth-grade football players from Derek's school! They saw him run back this way, and they're coming for us!"

I stared at Troy in shock. Like the poor bird which met an untimely demise and got an even weirder funeral, my friends and I were dead meat. "Call the police!" Troy screamed. "Grab your gun and run!"

The adrenaline kicked in, and I panicked. I ran as fast as my short legs would carry me. I darted through the back door for the phone with Troy in terrified pursuit. I dialled 911 and held the receiver to my ear. As the operator responded and asked me what my emergency was, I heard rubber squeal on the pavement as the bloodthirsty jocks pulled up near my parent's house. I impulsively hung up the phone without saying anything.

Troy and I didn't know what to do, so we ran down to the basement and hid for a short time. We re-loaded the pellet gun with ammunition while we were down there, just in case the jocks stormed inside for us. We waited a couple of tense minutes in the basement. All I could hear was my heart pounding through my chest. Then Troy suggested that we should go back out to see if Derek needed our help. Immediately, I regretted hanging up on the 911 call. Mustering our courage, we snuck outside to see if the teenagers had captured our guilty friend.

Troy and I cautiously crept into the ravine and followed the sound of the furious teens charging through the brush and trees, yelling threats. The four jocks finally caught up with Derek behind my neighbour's house and pinned my scrawny and terrified friend to the ground on his back. I was certain we were about to witness a homicide.

"Listen, you punk brat! Yeah, you better be afraid of us!" the angry ringleader shouted. "I should beat the snot out of you for pulling that stupid stunt! What were you thinking, you punk dweeb?"

Derek squirmed fearfully. "I—I'm—I'm sorry, guys. I know the stunt was messed up and stupid. I'm sorry! I promise this won't happen ever again. Please don't hurt me!"

The teens indulged in a few more minutes of poking, threatening, and taunting before they released him with a rough shove that sent him rolling in the dirt. Derek scrambled out of their reach and fled.

My parents found out an hour later about this strange event in our yard. My father grounded me and bought a gun safe that same week. My mother immediately phoned Derek's foster parents, who were oblivious to this drama.

The fact that those teenagers never harmed my

friend was a miracle. The fact that I was only grounded for two weeks was also remarkable. Those jocks had all of the muscles and all of the excuses to roll out their fists on my friend. I learned a great deal about grace and mercy that day from a messy, unexpected situation.

When we're stuck in predicaments and major mess-ups in our lives, we find ourselves in desperate need of help and childlike redemption. I struggle to wrap my head around the kind of grace God offers to us. The flavour of grace Jesus serves up is unfair and unbalanced in its delivery. He's always giving more than we deserve, and He never eases up, even when we keep screwing things up. Jesus said how this grace isn't something we can earn; we must humble ourselves to receive it.

Grace offers us more than we deserve so someday we can give back more than we can afford.

The Bible tells a story about a woman found guilty of adultery. The religious leaders brought her into the town square to stone her. Jesus confronted these men with a startling call, saying, "Let the one who has not sinned throw the first stone."

The religious leaders were dumbfounded. They had to drop their rocks. They all knew they had fallen short and had their own mess-ups, too. Only Jesus, being without sin, had the right to throw the first stone. He chose to extend mercy and grace to this sinful woman instead.

I've been guilty of bird-on-a-windshield moments in my lifetime. My life is littered with mess-ups and hang-ups, all the while learning to navigate my faith and the pathway of grace in Jesus. Impulsive actions and reactions are deeply woven into my story. I've hurt people I love due to my pride and selfishness. Sometimes I've been pinned to the ground, expecting to receive a swift blow for my sins and failures.

Two criminals hung next to Jesus on crosses at Golgotha. The first man mocked Jesus, daring Him to save all three of them. The second thief was remorseful and confessed to his crimes. He wept and told Jesus how he was worthy of the punishment he received. Jesus didn't offer judgement as He hung on the cross talking with this man. Instead, He offered him an eternity in paradise.

Through all my failures and mistakes, the only thing Jesus has ever offered me, as He has stood over my trembling, fearful self, was open arms of grace and love.

We're always expecting a painful blow when we know we deserve one. Jesus didn't want that for us. He laid His life down in our place so we would never experience the pain of judgement. Those of us who were trembling in our sin and failures now have a fresh start.

The way Jesus has shown His love for us is remarkable. We must choose to love others around us in remarkable, daring ways. Next time I find myself in the same position as those jocks, I'll remember the simple words of Jesus telling me to drop my stones and ease my grip of wrath on my victim.

Wrath makes sense in worldly terms. Some of us have thrown stones. Others of us have thrown birds. We've all thrown words in anger, too. Jesus calls our childlike selves to extend arms of love and mercy to people who don't deserve it—to live free from judgements and let Him do the judging instead.

Extending a God-sized love helps us grow into the kind of people Jesus has called us to be. Loving as Jesus did allows us to stay young at heart, too. The Bible explains how we should be quick to forgive others and slow to cast judgements. Children openhandedly forgive the wrongs done to them. We need to awaken our inner child's tender heart of kindness and practice the same acts of grace towards others.

Outstretched hands of grace and mercy help build the kingdom of heaven up around us—a kingdom everyone is invited to enter and enjoy.

Receiving and extending grace is the kind of courageous act that rekindles a spark of childlike hope and wonder in our now adult selves. Our lives need to be openhanded like those of young children. It's this resounding echo of laughter and hope that helps heal our broken-heartedness from a nagging world of hurts and wrongdoings.

I grew upset with my friend Derek for impulsively throwing the bird, but I accepted his apology. I didn't ever let him play with my BB gun ever again, though.

TEN

Aquatic Torture

*I used to think I had to do better to be accepted,
but now I know I'm accepted because Jesus did it all.*

I hated swimming lessons while growing up. I suffered from a deep-seated apprehension of large bodies of water and flutter-boards, thanks to some early childhood aquatic traumas. When I was three years old, my father took me on a summer day trip to Alberta Beach to go fishing. The shoreline was a harsh vertical cliff, appearing like the crest of Everest to my three-foot-tall self. My mother had decked me out appropriately in rubber boots and a second-hand raincoat.

A few minutes after my father planted me in a "safe" lakeside area, a quacking duck drifted its way over to greet us. I had never seen a real duck before; just Donald Duck in books and on television. My fascination consumed me, and I stretched out my tiny fingers toward its funny-looking neck. I thought a duck might make an excellent toddler ride.

My father should have had me tethered to an anvil. With my dad's attention diverted for only a second, I went for the swan dive, intending to land on the duck's back.

The duck wasn't rolling with my idea, and it swam off with an indignant squawk and flapping of wings as I took an untimely plunge into the icy deep. Our father-son date had barely begun, and my father hadn't had time to put on my life jacket yet.

From the murky depths of the lake, I heard a faint, hollow scream from the upper realm. Suddenly, a large hand splashed into the water and grabbed the back of my jacket, yanking me up. It felt like getting snatched out of a bad dream, or like those slingshot rides at the local carnivals.

My father placed me back on the shore a safe distance from the lake, soaking wet. He then guided me, dripping and shivering, to a picnic area. He wasn't upset with me; he was totally shocked, but at the same time, impressed with my attempt. He had foreseen the possibility of such a misadventure and had brought my Winnie the Pooh towel.

We stayed at the lake a while longer, catching and releasing some ugly, slimy fish. My father helped me cast the line in hopes of snagging a jackfish five times my size. We had a wonderful time together, and soon the shivers and cold memories subsided.

My mother didn't find out about my unscheduled nosedive until we got home. All I remember from my parents' conversation was hearing my mom exclaim, "We need to sign Justin up for swimming lessons immediately! We have to make sure this never happens again!"

I didn't understand what all of the swimming lesson fuss was about, but boy, was I going to find out!

Several years and many swimming classes later, when I was in grade five, my mother was getting ready to take me to Fountain Park Pool for my weekly swimming lesson. I was halfway through my badges and drawing ever closer to the sacred Bronze Medallion.

I viewed my swimming lesson as equivalent to a weekly waterboarding torture session. The drowning sensations I experienced during every class were enough to make anyone puke. I was prepared to go to extreme lengths to avoid being dragged to the pool.

On this occasion, while Mom was downstairs in the laundry room, I concocted a brilliant and disgusting plan to get out of that week's aquatic torture. I glanced over at the clock and gave myself T minus five minutes to carry out this masterful, dubious ploy. While my mother was loading my socks and undies into the washer, I was in the refrigerator gathering broccoli, soup, cheese, and anything else gross-looking I could find. I mixed this horrifying cocktail of ingredients into a bowl, then ran over to the main floor washroom. I began to cough and make hurling sounds as I slowly dumped the thick, green goo into the toilet bowl. I made sure I was loud enough for my mother to hear me in the laundry room. Sounds of coughing, fake crying, and yelling echoed through the bungalow until my mother rushed upstairs to see what all the noise was about. I appeared as weak and as miserable-looking as humanly possible, while I slumped over on the ground holding my belly. Though my performance was convincing, my mother wasn't buying it.

"Justin, get your swim trunks and towel. We are going to the pool," she ordered sternly. "Mom!" I whined. She ignored me. I slowly got up and slumped away to gather my trunks.

My Oscar-worthy performance might seem a little

over the top for a kid trying to get out of swimming lessons, but it certainly wasn't crazy for me. This hadn't worked. Next week, I would try siphoning the gas from my mother's Cavalier, or burning my swim shorts in an inferno.

The main reason I hated swimming lessons was that I was never properly taught one of the simplest concepts: exhaling underwater. I would multitask my arm flapping and leg fluttering, all the while holding my breath underwater. When I tilted my head to the side, I would breathe out and sometimes haphazardly gasp for air. This caused me to asphyxiate, and likely store too much carbon dioxide in my lungs. I would infrequently realize I needed oxygen and take sporadic breaths while my swimming technique flat-lined. I never thought to ask the teacher why it was hard for me to do a front crawl when the other kids tackled full laps with ease and determination. The swimming instructor never pinpointed my difficulty either. It's a miracle I passed the swimming levels that I did!

For me, the pool was a place of embarrassment, exhaustion, and defeat. I wish I could say I quickly figured out this whole exhaling underwater concept, but I honestly didn't realize my breathing hindrance until I watched the Summer Olympics on television in 2016. I was following one of Michael Phelps' final swims, and the underwater cameras caught an amazing perspective of the Olympian swimmer's stroke techniques and movements.

The transcendent realization struck me in a flash. Everything clicked. All those years of aquatic pain, torture, and heartache had finally come to an end. My fears of the infamous lane pool vaporized. I felt ready to cross the English channel that afternoon.

Swimming lessons were similar to the most uncom-
fortable and unnerving forms of religion to me. In the
pool, I was working my butt off, short of breath, barely
keeping my head above water. At the same time, I was
doing my best to say the right things, pray the right
prayers, and go to church each week. I struggled through
my faith journey, hoping religion would keep my salvation
secured. I wondered how everybody around me seemed to
be doing a lot better at life, religion, and swimming than I
was.

I failed to realize that there's a vast difference
between engaging Jesus in every part of your life and
trying to follow the rules while holding your breath. Religion has a funny way of aging us, sort of like smoking too
many cigarettes. Yuck.

Jesus wants us to let go of religion and take hold of
a relationship with Him instead. Jesus never forces us to
do twenty-five laps in a spiritual lane pool. He's the sort of
instructor who wants to make things simpler and more
fulfilling for us. He longs to remove the crippling, nauseat-
ing weight called religion from our chest.

Jesus was never about following rules and formu-
las, and He still isn't today.

What matters most to Him is the way we release our
lives to Him and realize how He is our breath and our life.

Religion leaves a bad taste in my mouth, and I bet a
lot of other people feel the same way. We construct our
own fake vomit plots in an attempt to stay clear of churches. We attempt to avoid religion, but while doing so, we
miss out on the real thing: a relationship with God. Many
adults get caught up in the lie that we have to work harder

and do more to be accepted by Jesus. We've been programmed to believe this fallacy since childhood. This constant motion and effort leave us gasping for breath and wanting nothing to do with church or Jesus.

Jesus isn't a grumpy swimming instructor blowing a whistle when we get things wrong. He's our loving Father. If we are willing to drop our religious mask, we can embrace the childlike wonder of enjoying the waters of joy again.

Many people have experienced their childlike faith get slowly swallowed by religion and the pastor criticizing their poor spiritual techniques. Life isn't about getting it right all the time, in spite of what religion tells us. We don't need this fake religious stuff to get to Jesus either. That veil of separation has been torn for good. We now have unhindered access to the kingdom of God.

Jesus comes alongside us in the midst of our brokenness, struggles, and failures, and teaches us to breathe out our anxieties and breathe in more of Him. Jesus beckons us to draw near to Him, rolling our burden onto His shoulders. We can find rest in His presence and freedom for our souls.

Religion robs the childlike wonder from our lives. It will asphyxiate us if we keep striving to be picture-perfect. Children don't concern themselves with getting religion right, or perfecting their swimming techniques either. They simply learn to embrace the true life and freedom Jesus offers them. Religion is a sad alternative in comparison to the childlike wonders of having a relationship with the living God.

We don't have to be ashamed if it's taken us longer than others to drop religion and get Jesus. Now we get to enjoy the breath of fresh air, knowing Jesus doesn't need us to get it right all the time. There's no Bronze Medallion badge reward for us either. Jesus is our matchless reward. The childlike joys of enjoying life with God is the real prize I'm after.

I'm still a little embarrassed about how long it took me to learn how to breathe out underwater. It's still fresh on my mind; but I can imagine Jesus looking at me from heaven, smiling and sending a holy fist bump down from His throne room. I can imagine Him graciously speaking hope over my failures and setbacks while motioning for me to keep moving forward. Jesus doesn't keep a long list of all the times we failed or got it wrong. He's more interested in us leaning in on Him and embracing the fact that He's proud of us, no matter the countless times we fail. Failure is inevitably an exciting part of the journey of our lives.

The enemy's mindset views failure as the end of us. The childlike mind view's our failures like the launching pad for our future successes. We must give ourselves extra grace and permission to trip and fall a few times as we learn to walk out this new life following after Christ. The beauty of this process, is the ability to fall forward, filled with hope and childlike wonder. Our childlike self celebrates other's failures, and believes for the best possible outcomes despite our worst mess-ups.

A couple of years ago, my family went canoeing on a mountain lake in Jasper. Due to a poor paddling stroke, I messed up big time, causing our canoe to tip over in the middle of the ice-cold lake! My parents and I tumbled into the bone-chilling, glacial waters. My mother frantically screamed in shock and horror. Our bodies were instantly stunned by the brisk, freezing waters.

Thanks to my numerous swimming lessons, I rescued my family and dog-paddled several hundred meters to shore, while holding onto the canoe. I'm proud to say we made it out alive that afternoon. As my family approached the shoreline, shivering and cold, and pulled ourselves out of the water, I cunningly turned around and asked my mother, "Is this why you made me take all those swimming lessons?"

ELEVEN

Snow Trails & Shortcuts

I used to despise maps because I thought I'd never get lost. Now I love God's directions because I've found my way home.

In the middle of winter, my father and I packed our sleeping bags and backpacks into his van for a weekend retreat. My eleventh birthday had just passed, and my father deemed me ready for a really manly weekend getaway to the mountains. We were heading to a father-son retreat in the Rocky Mountains with others from our church. I gazed out the passenger window, letting my imagination run loose as frosted trees twinkling in white zipped past outside. I envisioned slamming ice picks into the brittle faces of ice walls; barely summiting Mount Everest, and building giant bonfires in the great outdoors.

The rustic retreat centre stood in a forested area in the heart of the Canadian Rocky Mountains. Frontier Lodge was as remote and manly as you could get. I'm pretty sure the siding and shingles on the lodge were made of beef jerky and bacon.

The first morning at this winter camp came about extremely early. I was chipper with excitement, anticipating a larger than life-sized adventure. Eagerly, I scampered into the cafeteria to find a wonderful assortment of pancakes, bacon, sausages, and more bacon. Nothing beats the sweet and salty taste of maple-flavoured Canadian bacon. I sat down with some of my friends from church.

Soon after breakfast, the adventure guide, Chester, explained the wide array of activities scheduled for the day. Chester was a tall, skinny fellow, no more than twenty-five years old, who wore a 1980's Patagonia vest and a shaggy beard—a true mountaineer from the green knitted toque on his head to his worn, leather boots.

"And for our final activity option for the day, I am personally taking a crew of interested people snowshoeing up Coliseum Mountain. This will be a full- day trek! Do I have any volunteers?" Chester asked.

No one volunteered at first. Everyone was itching to try out faster, more exciting sports, like ice climbing or cross-country skiing. With genuine interest, I shot up my hand, hoping a few of my bunkmates would follow suit. Sure enough, six other hands popped up in the air. I rushed over to the other boys who agreed to take the trek, and we fought over who got to ride shotgun in the van. Then my father and I headed back to our cabin to put on our long underwear and sweaters. We were both excited for the mountaineering adventure ahead of us.

Fifteen minutes later, our crew piled into a fifteen-passenger van, and Chester drove us to the base of the mountain. He went over some safety instructions as we struggled to attach our snowshoes to our boots—the bindings were completely different than snowboard bindings. After we had wrestled with the unfamiliar straps for a few minutes, our guide ensured we had them strapped on tightly.

Our team indulged in an "all hands in" battle cry as we set off up the trail. The ascent was much less challenging than I had expected, in spite of the deep snow. Two hours quickly passed, and we neared the summit. Coliseum Mountain got its name because, unlike most peaks which are pointy at the top and pyramid-shaped, this particular mountain resembled the Coliseum in Rome. A giant dome of rock towered high above the tree line.

My father was pushing himself hard to keep up with our group of energetic pre-teens, and unlike a few other parents who gallantly concealed their fatigue, he was showing his pain. When our team finally passed the tree line and reached the top of the rocky dome, my father plonked down on the side of the trail in a hastily-constructed snow chair to let his heart rate level out.

"Finally, here we are, gentlemen. Great hustle! Welcome to the summit of the mountain," Chester shouted cheerfully. The group erupted in a cry of victory.

"Let's take a water and snack break, guys. You've earned it!" Chester proclaimed. Chester brought out a healthy supply of snacks for everyone to consume. We cracked open Ziploc bags of dried apples, granola bars, and tasty cheese sticks.

My father's energy did not return, in spite of the calories. He decided to stay back and catch up with our group after a few more minutes of rest. At first, I was apprehensive about leaving my father behind. But he assured me and Chester he would be okay for a little while on his own. I knew I would be fine with the gang and our homely guide, and I was too young to fully realize how wildly unsafe it was for Chester to leave my father alone on the top of the mountain. Our team waved goodbye to my father. Chester rallied the troops and gave us further instructions.

"It looks like the weather is taking a turn for the worse, gentlemen. Let's head back down the trail. A snow system is rolling into the valley, and we need to get ahead of it."

All the snacking gave us renewed energy and enthusiasm. The downward slope was gradual. We attempted to lunge and slide across the snow, but snowshoes aren't skis, and we laughed and joked as a few of us face-planted in the deep, fresh powder.

After twenty minutes of trekking through the snow, our guide paused and made an impulsive decision. Chester motioned to the southwest, down a narrow break in the trees.

"I think I see a sweet shortcut for us, guys. It should save us a lot of time so we can beat the weather rolling in. Let's go this way!"

Trusting Chester's knowledge of the mountain, we plunged into the ankle-deep snow of the ill-frequented trail. Eventually, with no sign of civilization in sight, Chester's strides slowed, and I began to second-guess his decision.

"Hey, Chester, is everything okay, man?" I nervously asked him.

"Umm—yeah I think so..." His eyes filled with worry. " We may have gone a little bit too far to the south. I don't see the next set of switchbacks up ahead." I stared up at him blankly.

Our group halted, trying to process the fact that we were lost on a mountainside with a snowstorm blowing in. "Man, we are so dead!" a young boy said.

It appeared we had little choice but to continue down the mountain. Retracing our steps at this point would have added a lot of time and effort to our journey. Another thirty minutes went by, and it felt like we were gradually making some progress. The only direction any of us could tell clearly was down, but no one knew whether we were heading toward the lodge or away from it.

My mind began racing, my thoughts tumbling over one another in a disordered cacophony. "Our guide is an idiot. I sure hope we have more apple slices left. My dad will never be able to find us. Look tough, Justin. They usually eat the scrawniest hiker first."

By this time, we were far down the trail, and we had a great view of the dome of rock at the top of the mountain. I had an idea to look back up at the mountain and see if we recognized the view, like the view from the parking lot. Re-aligning ourselves with the correct view might help us find our way back home.

I remembered one of King David's psalms explaining how he would often look up to the mountains in times of trouble, and ask where his help came from. He declared how his help came from God, the maker of the heavens and the earth.

Chester did not intend to lead us astray by blazing his own trail down the mountain. He meant well, and his impulsive action was just like what many of us do in our own lives. We often know the way we should go, but sometimes we try to find shortcuts to get to our destination quicker. If we're not careful, like our guide, Chester, we can end up way off track and lose the course entirely. At this point, we have two options: we can keep walking blindly down our own path, pretending things will get better, or we can look up to the mountain of God and ask for help.

No matter how lost we get, we always have the view of the mountaintop of God in the distance, permitting us a heaven-sent childlike perspective. This mountain is our true guide, our northern compass, our refuge in times of trouble.

As children, we are filled with wide-eyed wonder. We never question the idea of God when we're told about His existence at a young age. We're told of this wonderful summit, and we eagerly strap on our snowshoes in anticipation for the journey of life. Children have an uncanny ability to see the kingdom of heaven off in the distance, like a mountaintop, which fills them with joy and laughter. As we journey further on the trail, we lose track of the right path to follow. Failures, brokenness, and negative relationships pull us off course, distracting us from our prized destination.

Too often, we follow an inexperienced guide, such as a celebrity or a friend, who is unknowingly leading us astray. The further we travel from the mountain with them, the harder it gets to see it in the distance, to find our true north, our way back home. Jesus says how He has set a path of life before us. A line in the book of Proverbs says there's a way which seems right to a man, but in the end, leads to destruction.

I'm not willing to be led down a path like this any longer. It can only end in calamity. Sure we'll be tempted to make our own shortcuts from time to time, but we know inside it's not the best idea, due to our lack of navigational knowledge.

Some adults think they have everything together.

But that's just pride telling God to hand over the map and let us lead for a while. The Bible says how pride comes before a fall. You never know how far you'll fall until it happens to you. We must keep our sights set on course, on the map which lays out this path of life for us to follow: the Word of God.

God sees the bigger picture of our lives when often all we can see is the next patch of spruce trees in the distance. Rushing ahead of God's plan for us only slows us down in the end.

We see our neighbours and families with high paying jobs, fancy SUV's and white picket fences, and something attracts us to this path of comfort and safety. But comfort can be crippling. Comfort can keep us from our God-designed destinies. Comfort can feed into the crutch of pride, which leaves us leading self-centred lives where God has no place. Something born deep inside us, beyond the thrones of comfort, calls us out onto the pathway of adventure, to pursue the tremendous mountaintops of the kingdom of heaven.

Many people desperately chase after luxuries that will never satisfy their inner child's inherent longings. Our young minds once overflowed with unspeakable treasured dreams and childlike fantasies, longed to grow and impact our future selves. Someone tricked us into believing that we outgrew these dreams, somewhere between passing our drivers training and receiving our first credit card in the mail.

Jesus calls us to a different path, one that requires a childlike heart and perspective to come out and play again. He calls us to take the narrow road: it's the path that leads to life and adventure with Him. This road flows in complete opposition with the systems of our present world. The system of 'normal' plans to keep our childlike selves imprisoned and contained. Why not go after your dreams with fearless enthusiasm. What do we really have to lose? I often hear people say how our lives need to have more balance. I'm convinced that we don't need more balance in our lives, we just need more of Jesus. He offers us the courage to live a life outside of the boundaries of others ordinary, average expectations.

Jared Angaza, a world-changing philanthropist, states: "We can either be normal, or live in wonderland. We can't have both." Jared and I both choose the adventure of life in wonderland. We hope you will too.

As our team hiked onwards, I found much comfort in these words from Jesus, confident that we would soon find our way back home with God's help.

The parking lot we desperately hoped to find finally came into view. Chester threw his hands in the air and gave a mighty shout of victory. Our crew smiled and hugged each other with overwhelming joy and relief. We were grateful to have made it back home, but I was missing my father a lot. I was hoping he had beaten us back to the van. As I approached the vehicle, my father greeted us, relaxing happily in the passenger seat.

Even though we had every right to be upset with Chester, we decided to cut him some slack. He probably could have lost his job for such a mishap, especially if he had turned us all into ice cubes. Instead, we gave him fist bumps and smiles with a "Never do this again, or else!" wink and nudge.

On the drive back to the lodge, we laughed and reflected on our day as a group, and all I could think about as we drove down the mountain road was how the other guys who had stayed at the lodge were never going to believe our story.

TWELVE

Sketchbooks
& Safety Scissors

I used to think I had try harder to be creative.
Now I know being creative is a part of me.

I spent most of my preschool years on the floor of my crafting room. My elbows and wrists would get sore after countless hours on the linoleum. I had an arts and crafts obsession. My parents couldn't afford the amount of paper I required for my drawing exploits.

My father had an ancient 1980s printer at his office: Gutenberg Press Model Two. The paper was coiled with tiny holes on each side which guided it through metallic gears on the printer. This massive printing machine would always spit out an extra page or two after printing out sales reports, which were kept in a bag to be thrown out at the end of each work week. My father didn't want to see this paper go to waste, so he brought the giant bag home to support my sketching endeavours.

These sheets were four times the size of the stand-ard printer paper we use today. Light green lines adorned one side of the page, and the other side of each sheet was blank. My father knew my frequent drawing times brought our home much peace and quiet, and he wanted to encourage me as much as he could!

I drew everything under the sun: cars, Disney characters, castles, time machines, and Batman. My fascination with drawing started with those incredible, scented, coloured markers. I don't think you can purchase them anymore due to far too many children lodging the coloured tips in their noses. I had a preschool playmate who would sniff the red marker like his life depended on it. He thought he would snort out an actual strawberry if he sniffed hard enough. This kid even licked the marker once or twice. I tried that too. They didn't taste as amazing as they smelled.

I grew up in the age of the prehistoric Macintosh computer, which is nothing like the iMac desktops or the MacBook Pros we see today. This model of the Macintosh weighed a solid two-hundred pounds. You had to wear sunglasses when you hit the power button, due to a dazzling flash of light from the monitor which shocked your retinas. Before wifi, all we had was dial-up internet. The internet signal buffer sounded like you were dialling to outer space from the Starship Enterprise.

If I wasn't drawing on the floor, I would hold my computer mouse in a death grip as I navigated my way into my next pixelated drawing. I wanted to design colourful and classy skateboard shoes. My initial inspiration came from a pair of runners I saw at the local skate shop. I made a creative logo and customized dozens of designs. I spent numerous cold winters completely captivated by these computerized images. Bold colours, intriguing shapes, geometric logos, and stylish patterns bubbled out of my creative mind in a never-ending flow of ideas and inspiration. I soon discovered that the beautiful imagery I had painted in my heart could take form in the world around me. I was ready to take my ingenious creations off the screen and into the prototype phase for a summer 1996 release date. This called for rubber, fabric, and some fancy safety-scissor engineering.

My mother heard about a new outlet store called the Imagination Market from my friend Lindsay's mom, who explained how the place was jam-packed with creative crafting supplies just for kids. This store was giving bulk art supplies away for pennies on the dollar. Lindsay and I were inseparable childhood friends. We were both wildly creative and got along really well. We couldn't get enough art supplies to meet the demands of our overactive imaginations.

In short order, my mother called for Lindsay and me to jump in the station wagon, and we headed to the store. After a ten-minute drive which felt like an hour, I ran into the store and greeted one of the clerks at the counter. The tall lady at the front desk gave me a giant bag and said I could fill it to the top with any items I wanted. She explained how anything I could fit into the bag would cost only two dollars. My eyes widened in utter disbelief. My shoe drawings were really going to come to life!

I enthusiastically flowed between the aisles of bins, gazing on all of the childlike treasures. I discovered colourful wires, styrofoam chunks, pipe cleaners, fabrics, coroplast, lego pieces, and shiny foil paper. The place had everything I could ever hope to find in a crafting superstore.

After an hour of shopping, I finished stuffing my bag full of creative items and carefully hauled the materials to the front counter to pay. I unloaded a pocketful of change and methodically counted out eight quarters. I landed a jackpot of a deal. This store was as miraculously fantastic as Willy Wonka's Chocolate Factory. I can remember humming the familiar song from the 1970s film, where Mr. Wonka sings, "Come with me, and you'll see, a world of pure imagination."

I hummed that song all the way out of the store. My friend, Lindsay, nearly teared up, overwhelmed with child-like joy and wonder. Her imagination had found a new home. I gave her a big hug, and we smiled at each other. We gripped our paper shopping bags with both hands and followed my mother to the car.

This was a remarkable religious experience for us. Our sanctuaries were our crafting rooms, and we gave our daily offerings of worship with our crayons, safety scissors, and pencils. This store became our church, where we came for our weekly gatherings. One might think a weekly trip to the crafting market was excessive, but it was a necessary endeavour for us!

I had a shoe store to launch, and Lindsay was building her own time machine. Summer flew by as we worked on our creative projects, although my shoes never made it to skateboard shops like I had planned. I lacked the necessary capital to start my global enterprise. It didn't bother me that I never started my shoe company. The innovative process was the real thrill that I pursued and found joy in.

Creativity feels like heaven on earth for me, and the Imagination Market fanned the flames burning in my childlike heart. In those early years, I could imagine or become anyone I wanted to be. Sometimes I wanted to be the next Picasso, and paint a flawless landscape of Batman's Wayne Manor. After my family acquired the puter, I wanted to be the next C.S. Lewis, and complete my fantasy novel, full of wizards, dragons, and unspeakable danger.

We all grow up too fast. It's easier to deny our creativity than to engage and unlock it. We flippantly trade in our creative destinies for monthly mortgage payments, credit card debt, and menial careers. We think what we are doing with our lives is noble and admirable, but all we're doing is sacrificing our childhoods on the altar of the American Dream.

We were all born to become someone truly remarkable, but we somehow forget this along the way. The trials of life kick the wonder out of us before we dare to kick back.

I had a few upsets growing up. While my parents were loving and supportive of my sister and me, they would often become stressed out and frustrated with each other.

Instead of resolving conflicts appropriately, they chose to throw harsh words and raise their voices at one other, leaving my sister and me caught in the crossfire. My sister and I often hid out in the basement while the echoes of their violent shouting reverberated through the thin walls.

The enemy, Satan, was attempting to pitch his tent full of unrest and anxiety in my childhood.

I chose to occupy those far-too-frequent moments of fear and uncertainty with my crafts and crayons. On one occasion, I sat next to my sister clutching a handful of markers while we both cowered in the crafting room in the basement. Trying to tune out the shouting, I created a green, sharp-toothed monster out of a discarded pizza box.

I desperately wanted this scary monster to defeat the anger raging in my home and end my parents' fighting.

I comforted myself with art and creativity throughout my childhood, praying my creations would be bold enough to kick out this enemy once and for all.

We can craft our way into a greater glimpse of heaven on earth. Jesus doesn't judge our drawings when we draw outside of the lines and boxes either.

Jesus told His disciples if anyone caused the little ones who believed in Him to stumble, it would be better for them to be trapped at the bottom of the sea with a millstone chained to their neck. Those words are harsh, but I think I know what He was getting at. He's stating that if anyone tells the children to drop their crayons and lose their small glimpses of heaven on earth, they will be in big trouble.

Jesus spoke sternly to the religious leaders of His time and told them that the inside of their lives looked like whitewashed tombs. He said there isn't much left to work with below the surface. I would not want the inside of my life looking like a tomb, complete with terrifying corpses! He's saying those Pharisees let their dreams, ambitions, creativity, and childlike wonder die over time.

Creativity is one of the weapons of heaven the enemy can't stand up against. God created us to create beauty in the world around us. When we fight with the creativity stored up inside us, we are fighting to bring a little bit more of heaven down to earth.

The famous Picasso said, "Every child is an artist. The real problem is staying an artist when you grow up." The systems around us are trying their best to yank us out of this kingdom of creativity and imagination. We have to be taught to grow up. It doesn't happen naturally like you might think. Growing up stomps all over our childlike creativity, and our dreams and ambitions get ridiculed and defeated as we are dragged out of childhood. It can feel like we have no choice but to conform to the broken systems that keep our childlike wonder shut away and silenced.

In a world telling us we need more money, what we really need is more meaning.

This world doesn't grant us permission to stay childlike, but the only permission I'll ever need comes from the only person whose opinion matters to me: Jesus. He gives us all the permission we'll ever require to stay young at heart.

The famous writer C.S. Lewis put it plainly. "When I became a man, I put away childish things, including the fear of childishness and the desire to be very grown up."

Lewis never let the feeble opinions of others, or his own fears, stunt his childlike growth in pursuing inventive works. He found a way to uphold his childlike nature in the pursuit of creativity throughout his adult life. Lewis penned some of the most marvellous essays and novels this world has ever seen. He brought the magical world of Narnia to life in the minds of children and adults every-where. We could learn a thing or two from his unwavering zest for life and artistic expression. The limitless fountain of wonder Lewis drew from for his inspiration is available to all of us.

The devil longs to halt our creative juices, because he doesn't want heaven to invade this battlefield on earth. He doesn't want us to invent a medical machine, or write a book which could change the world for the better. What would the earth look like if each and every person embraced their creative destinies and offered themselves up for the betterment of our society?

The apostle Paul said, "we are God's masterpieces; created in Christ's image to do good works, which He prepared in advance for us to do." God wrote a piece of heaven into your life from day one, which only you can let out. Heaven wrote a song into our hearts that only we can sing. God is writing a story with the ways He has gifted you and me, and we need to live it out loud. A hurting world is waiting for you to become something extraordinary.

We've all had a passion for a creative pursuit that we haven't touched in years. It's time to pick up the old dusty guitar, put on your tap dancing shoes, sign up for art classes, or begin writing that novel. We were made with extraordinary potential and complex design. A creative gallery of wonder is waiting to be released by the underrated artisans of our world. When we fail to create according to how God has gifted us, the world misses out on something significant that we were meant to contribute.

Our next creation could cure cancer, solve a crisis, or inspire a generation. We must take a risk, fight off our inner mind's resistance, and let our art take form around us.

Let's fill up our mental bags of imagination with pipe cleaners, foam boards, fabrics, and wires. Let's sing a song of hope until the whole world is singing with us. We will create a beautiful world of childlike wonder together. The Imagination Market is where we all belong.

THIRTEEN

Parkades & Hacksaws

I used to hide my past in the basement, but Jesus gave me the courage to break in and learn from my mistakes.

"Do you really think this is a good idea?" Shawn nervously voiced a question my friends asked all-too-frequently during my pre-teen years.

Mischief and satisfaction of curiosity were our chief aims, and today was no exception. My three friends and I unwound the long hose on the fire extinguisher tank as we carried the contraption out of my father's tool shed. The sixty-pound extinguisher required all of our strength to haul around.

Shawn was the new kid in the neighbourhood. He didn't grow up on a skateboard like the rest of my friends and me, so instead of skateboard stunts, we were trying to find another way to officially welcome him into our crew. My friend, Donovan, and I figured that shooting a fire extinguisher at him would be an appropriate act of initiation, and Shawn was the type of kid to say yes to anything, even before he actually knew what he was agreeing to.

A few of my friends stood downwind from the fire extinguisher as Shawn timidly entered the small shed. We carefully shut him in and pushed the extinguisher hose inside through a small opening in the door. We all held our breath. Would Shawn live to tell the tale? He hollered at us, his voice muffled behind the door, confirming that his snowboard goggles were strapped comfortably around his face. A shot to the eye with that fire retardant would have sent him to the hospital otherwise, and we were far too responsible to allow something like that to happen.

"Three, two, one, go!" I shouted.

KABOOM! A puff of powder blew out of the crack around the shed door, then a whistling noise barrelled out of the large extinguisher cauldron. I clenched the hose firmly to keep control of it as a thick, foamy blast of retardant spewed powerfully into the shed, from which the boys and I heard a sudden howling sound. After a few moments, the extinguisher was completely discharged, and we listened for some feedback from our poor pledge, Shawn. A strangled, gurgling sound came from within the shed. I opened the door, and my foam covered friend stumbled out onto the grass. We had a survivor! Barely. He appeared thirty percent larger, and resembled a fluffy, white cloud of tortured juvenile.

My friends and I weren't bad children. We were just far too curious and hungry for adrenaline-induced adventure—even if, all too often, that adventure resulted in us running for our lives.

I lived near a large, abandoned, three-story parkade. The lower levels were formerly used as a car park, and the top floor had been a tennis court in a previous life. The parkade was owned by the adjacent mall. The mall security team regularly patrolled the old parkade, looking for troublemakers.

My friends and I spent a lot of time cruising around the parkade and the tennis courts on our skateboards on long summer days. We made bets on how quickly the security guards would meet us there. Often, Doug, the chief security guard, would forcefully kick us off the property only minutes into our skateboarding adventures. But we kept coming back. Breaking the rules and hanging out where we weren't allowed was exhilarating!

On the tennis court level was a padlocked stairwell door with a "No Trespassing" sign stapled to the wall. Our crew had heard many horrific stories from older boys about why this stairwell was locked. Some spoke of murders, others of tunnels, hidden treasure, or secret underground military bases. My friends and I poked around that mysterious door for several summers before our curiosity finally got the best of us. We were going to break in.

We gathered up a hacksaw and some crowbars from my father's tool shed while he was at work. We hid the tools in our backpacks as we skateboarded a few blocks down to the parkade.

My friend, Donovan, pulled the hacksaw out as a few other boys surveyed the perimeter for guards. We wasted no time beginning to saw through the metal chains that were wrapped through the handle hole and fastened through a hole drilled in the doorway frame.

The cutting went surprisingly fast, and before we knew it, we had broken through the chains. We swiftly removed them, and a cloud of dust spewed into the open air as we cracked open the creepy door. The space was full of cobwebs.

My four friends and I cast rocks to see which two of us would keep a lookout, and which of us would bravely descend into the unknown to explore. After a few moments of fuss, Donovan and I were picked to enter the foreboding stairwell.

I entered the dark passageway first, sparking my flashlight on. Donovan followed close behind me. As we approached the bottom of the first flight, we found a graphic graffiti mural plastered across the walls. This image reminded me of the older boys' stories about the danger and past crimes that took place in this stairwell. Our fascination and curiosity grew as we continued down the stairs. Anxiety rattled our spirits as we inched ever closer to the bottom, hoping there was a bottom to find.

I wish I could tell you we found hidden treasure, a pirate's skeleton, or an entrance to Narnia at the bottom of that stairwell, but we never made it all the way down. The boys on lookout duty spotted Doug, the security guard, walking across the mall parking lot toward the parkade. This would only give us a minute or two for a speedy getaway on our skateboards. The boys on the roof shouted down the stairwell, and we immediately took flight back up the dark stairs.

Someone secured the stairwell with a stouter chain, and we never tried to break in again.

Years later, the parkade was bulldozed and an apartment complex sprang up to replace it, but I still held the memories of playing in the concrete wasteland. The interesting thing about this brand new apartment struc-ture was that it remained empty as well. Maybe the units were severely overpriced, or perhaps the company didn't do enough market research on the community. I'd like to think that the land was cursed and forever uninhabitable. The fact was that even though this new shell of a structure looked a lot prettier on the outside, the inside remained as empty as that old parkade.

The parkade-turned-vacant-apartment reminds me of my own life. I've tried to remodel and rebuild my life on my terms from time to time. Sometimes it's easier to cover up the damage of our broken childhoods with a demolition, or to chain shut the areas of our hearts where the memories of past hurts and traumas live.

So many of us have this idea that if we only build something bigger and better to replace our childlike selves, then we will be happier in the end. All too often, we are left with a freshly built structure that is lifeless and empty.

Jesus told a story about empty houses. He said that if we're not careful, when our house remains empty, unwelcome company will make its way in and find a new home. These uninvited guests can resemble things like selfishness, pride, anger, bitterness, fear and childishness.

If we permit bad things to move into our hearts and lives, it becomes much easier to want to demolish our human structures trying to get rid of the invaders. Better to ensure that we allow good things to take up residence in our hearts and lives instead.

Attempting to rebuild our lives on a weak foundation is no better than building our house on sand. Jesus calls us to build our lives on the firm ground of faith and trust in Him.

Jesus told a parable of two neighbours who chose to build their homes on different foundations. The first neighbour built his house on the rock, a firm foundation, while the second built his home on sand. A huge, tropical storm sprang up and hit their neighbourhood hard, totally destroying the house built on sand. The second man's home was a write-off.

When it comes to broken-down homes, or broken-down lives, there are always fair reasons for wanting to tear down our past and rebuild something to replace our childhoods. Maybe the memory you want to let go of was the loss of a loved one. Perhaps it was the first time you were picked on by a bully at school, or the time your parents got a divorce.

The tragedy of living abandoned parkade-like lives is that there are always stairwells chained shut with "No Trespassing" signs on the doors. These stairwells contain the stories and the meaning that we've been aching to rediscover all along. Opening the padlocked doors of our hearts is where we can find the answers to life's troubling questions. It's where we can discover a fresh perspective on challenging circumstances. It's where we can find healing and resolve from our past hurts.

Often, we can impulsively act out of childishness in our own lives, similar to covering our friends in fire retardant in the tool shed. Instead of cleaning up these messes of our past, we choose to ignore the obvious need for soap and a garden hose. We close up the doors on damaged relationships, deciding not to deal with the consequences of our actions toward others.

We fear letting others into these spaces, showing them our inner demons, our pain, our hurts, and regrets. Sometimes, we even hold our childlike selves hostage at the bottom of these dark stairwells, due to past trauma, rejection, or loss of innocence.

There are countless reasons why we would want to lock the doors of our hearts and throw away the key. We often assume life will be easier if we leave our pain in the dark and dusty cobweb-ridden basement where we think it belongs.

Jesus doesn't want to see our childlike nature get torn down or abandoned. He especially doesn't want to see our inner child's faith meet an untimely demise. He is calling us to embark on the heist of the century, to rediscover and rescue our inner child from captivity. This childlike heist requires risk, curiosity, and adventure if we hold any chance of successfully pulling off this grand caper.

The rooms of our past that we fear to enter surely hold the buried treasures of wonder that we desperately seek. Heaven is peering through the clouds with anticipation, hoping that we will have the courage to cut the locks on the chains that have been holding our childlike selves in bondage for so long. Jesus doesn't want to see the very foundation of who He made us to be fall victim to the destruction of a wrecking ball or a jackhammer.

Many of us have been hiding in the basements of our lives for far too long, and it's time for a jailbreak. It's time to muster up our childlike curiosity and take down the locks with a hacksaw.

Take a giant, childlike leap of faith and allow Jesus to break down the barriers and doors that are stopping Him from getting into our lives. Everywhere there is darkness, cobwebs, and decay, the light of Christ can expose it and restore us on the inside out. There's no wall He won't tear down if it means getting more of Him. There's no chain or lock God won't cut through if it means rescuing our childlike self from the enemy's demolition plans. Only Jesus can restore and renovate our broken hearts and make our abandoned childhood basements livable again. We need not fear the enemy's shouts and taunting remarks

remarks when we delve into the basement of our lives. The devil might shout accusations and tell us to leave the premises, but we can ignore him completely. The enemy knows that if we keep going down the dark stairwell, we may find a piece of ourselves we've been missing all along.

When we step into the basements of our lives, full of wonder and curiosity, Jesus promises us that He will be our guiding light along the way. Never let a few cobwebs or security guards stop you on your quest to rescue your childlike self hiding in the darkness.

FOURTEEN

Dinosaurs and the Disappearing Dresser

I used to hide the past because it hurt.
Now I embrace it because the pain brought peace.

My parents and I decided to register me at Sir George Simpson Junior High School for seventh grade. My transition from homeschooling to the classroom was enjoyable and smooth. I quickly made many friends and found my place as the class clown.

In the spring of that school year, my entire class went on a thrilling road trip to the Royal Tyrrell Dinosaur Museum in Drumheller, Alberta. I felt excited and refreshed to get out of the confines of the classroom and explore to my heart's content. My first field trip without my mother's eagle-eyed supervision was the adventure of a lifetime.

Our class hiked in the Badlands and even observed a fossil dig site. Being in the great, prehistoric outdoors satisfied a longing in my childlike soul.

The dinosaur exhibits transported me to another world entirely, a place where I was the Indiana Jones-like leader of an expedition in a tropical, foreign land. My creative mind carried me far off to a time when the Tyrannosaurus Rex still ruled the earth. I imagined carrying my hefty dinosaur gun slung over my back as I ascended the rainforest ravines in the scorching jungle summer. One of the teachers had to call for my attention as my mind continued to wander.

"Justin, is everything okay? You're falling behind the group. Please catch up!" she encouraged.

I snapped out of my daydream and ran ahead to join the class. We spent an hour surveying the exciting exhibits throughout the museum. The impressive, towering displays awed and terrified me, and I was glad when the tour guide reassured me I wouldn't be meeting a T-Rex on my way home from school.

The day trip turned out to be one for the history books. A friend of mine found a real fossil in a rock, and I impressed a few girls from class with my growling-dinosaur impressions. The eventful day flew by quicker than we had anticipated. Before we had time to dig up a dinosaur, the teachers herded us back onto the bus.

A three-hour journey on the school bus flashed by as my friends and I played a card game in the back corner, and before I knew it, the vehicle was pulling up outside the school. My mother greeted me on the sidewalk as soon as I disembarked. On the drive home, she asked me about the dinosaur museum. I filled her in on the details of my day and asked her whether raptors were still a legitimate threat. She assured me they were no longer a concern.

I was beyond excited to rush inside the house, give my father a giant hug, and tell him all about the giant snake I wrangled off my head. He must have been away on an errand though, because his work truck wasn't in the driveway. I opened the front door and called out "hello?"

to check if anyone was home. No one responded. I whipped off my skate shoes and made a dash for my room.

I dropped my backpack on the floor, along with my baseball cap. Before I had left that morning, my dad had assured me that he would be there to hear about my adventures when I returned. Where was he? I strolled back to the front entrance. "Hey, Mom, do you know where dad is? He said he would be here when I got home."

My mother looked a bit flustered. "I'm not sure where he is, Justin. He must be out running errands." I wanted to believe her, but I had a bad feeling inside, and I was curious to find out what was going on. My heart pounding strangely in my chest, I snuck down the hall to my parents' room and nudged the door open with my foot. I knew I shouldn't enter their room without permission, but I could scan the area for abnormalities. Maybe Dad was napping? The bed was empty. All of a sudden, something caught my eye—or rather, its absence did. My father's dresser had vanished!

Disregarding the entry prohibition, I walked over to the place where the dresser had sat and put my sleuthing skills to work. I examined the floor closely and found a dusty square outline of the disappearing dresser.

I was baffled and confused, and my mind whirled with possibilities. Perhaps a tractor beam had vaporized my father's dresser. Maybe he had decided to invest in a new dresser and was picking one up at IKEA. Or my worst nightmare was unfolding: he had moved out and left my family. I refused to endorse option three, so I ran back to the living room to inform my mother of my startling discovery.

"Mom, where's Dad? Where is his dresser?" I asked.

She blanched. She rushed to the phone and quickly dialled my father's cellphone number. After a few moments of waiting for him to pick up, she placed the handset back on the cradle and began to weep. I knew something was terribly wrong. Where was my father? Where was his truck? Why wasn't he answering his phone? Why wasn't he here with us when I desperately needed him?

My racing thoughts made sleep difficult that night. Had my father decided to desert my family? Tears filled my eyes as a dirty feeling of frustration buried my childlike hopes alive. I felt abandoned at that moment, angry and confused, filled with a million questions and zero answers. I bottled up my emotions like an overfilled CO_2 canister ready to explode.

It felt like walls of darkness were closing in on my life. Pain became my only companion in those wakeful, weary moments, alone in my room. I cried myself to sleep that night, but my dreams matched my nightmarish reality.

In the morning, I slipped out of my bed and wandered into the kitchen. My mother was standing at the counter, and she greeted me with the old, familiar "we need to talk" look on her face. She sat me down at the table to update me on the situation.

"Justin, I spoke to your father this morning, and he explained that he decided to move out yesterday afternoon." A sob caught in my mother's throat and her fearful eyes glistened with unshed tears.

I was speechless. I felt abandoned and angry all at once. My mind whirled back to the previous weeks, when my parents' arguments were swiftly worsening. I could still hear the crack of my father's hand across my mother's face when he slapped her during a heated shouting match at the front door. I wanted to defend her; I couldn't bear to see my father hurt her, but I was powerless to intervene.

When the officer had arrived and sat me in the back of a police cruiser while he went inside to deal with my parents, I tried to block out all thought of the physical altercation. I could make my grand escape. The keys were in the ignition. I could have high-tailed my way out of there and started a new life as the world's youngest outlaw.

Tears welled up and stained my cheeks as I sat in the car completely shattered inside. I was sick and tired of picking sides, of being caught in the middle. Why couldn't my parents just get along? They were broken and selfish; why did I have to pay the price?

"Justin? You'll still see Dad."

My mother's trembling voice drew me back to the present. I stared at her, but I couldn't accept her gentle words. Seeds of anger sprouted in my heart and infected my childlike spirit with terribly twisted roots of bitterness. Those roots sprang into an internal cactus plant, its spines slicing at my childlike wonder. I began to lose pieces of who I was.

I wore my anger like a grown up gangster wearing a porcupine quill jean jacket, along with the constant, nagging thought that my dad leaving was my fault. I built coffin walls around the truth to hide it from my friends, and buried my father's departure six feet underground, fearing embarrassment and rejection. Weeks passed by where I hid the pain of my father's exit under truckloads of dirt. I was hoping I could pretend forever. I convinced my friends that my father was often away on business trips.

I became an excellent con man after a while. I had an excuse for everything. The lie held up longer than I had expected. It had time to decay and fossilize. But after far less than sixty-five million years, the dinosaur-sized secret began to surface.

Those bones and crumbling vertebrae began to poke out of the earth, and I started tripping over my lies. My mother mentioned me going to my father's house in front of my friends, and I couldn't conceal the secret anymore. I needed to tell them the truth.

Nobody is excluded from the pain of family hurts and separations. Kids often feel the brunt of warfare early on, and suffer loss, bruises, and shell shock along the way.

In the face of family traumas and violence, we close ourselves in and switch into self-preservation mode. We take our shovels to the sandpit when nobody is watching and bury those raw emotions, feelings, and tough memories as deep down as possible. We often keep these skeletons buried as we move into adulthood, leaving our dreams and hopes six feet under along with them.

Through all of the suffering and heartache, pain has a purpose, even when we feel as though life's struggles are meaningless. Jesus has the power to bring a fresh childlike perspective of hope on tough circumstances. He longs to form beauty out of the messes of our lives.

I started excavating those buried bones slowly but surely over time. I dug up the memories of my brokenness with shovelfuls of redemptive hope. I brushed at the edges of the bones within the ground and asked myself why I fought to hide the truth for so long. This process wasn't easy. I had to take a risk and be vulnerable with the people who cared about me and open up the dig site in my heart for others to explore and cultivate.

Freedom is revealed in the excavation process, and pain is a vital part of our story. If we don't experience pain and confront the traumas of our past, we never really grow into who God made us to be.

The paintbrush strokes of trouble in our lives are a part of the masterpiece Jesus is forming. He takes the broken pieces and constructs beauty out of chaos. We need to pray for heaven's perspective to view life in this remarkable way and believe that He can restore all things for His glory. The Bible says that God makes all things work together for good, even our struggles and challenges.

This endearing childlike perspective emphasizes the beauty written through all of our stories, even the ones we wish we weren't part of. What if the key to our destinies is locked six feet under in the backyards of our childhoods? What if a pirate's chest full of hope is stored up for those who believe in miracles and redemption?

I used to think my childlike wonder had succumbed to extinction, but what if it could come alive?

I now believe our pain has a purpose, and His name is Jesus.

The prophet Ezekiel had a vivid dream where he saw a field of dry, weary bones. He asked God to breathe new life into the wasteland of death and decay. With one breath from the creator, those bones suddenly rose up and became a living army, ready for battle. God brought new life to Ezekiel's hopeless story.

My parents eventually decided to reconcile their marriage after several years of separation. They found the strength in God to breathe new life into their seemingly hopeless situation. My father moved back home.

I believe in miracles today because seeing my parents' marriage restored is one of the biggest miracles of all. They had to pick up their own set of tools and work on the excavation process of redemption in their relationship together. Though their marriage is less than perfect, they have found new strength to move forward through vulnerability and reliance on Jesus.

Jesus is calling our childlike selves to rise up from the dirt of our messy, broken childhoods. He is calling us out of the grave, out of the grips of extinction, into new life in Him. I used to think Jesus made bad people good. But now I know He makes dead things come alive.

FIFTEEN

Hell House

I used to be scared of the dark,
but then the light of Jesus shone through.

My family attended a vibrant church in the west end of Edmonton for most of my childhood. Each Sunday morning, the church was filled with a lot of people cheering, dancing, and singing along with the loud music. I spent countless hours racing around the foyer, eating far too many Sunday school snacks, and learning how to politely treat strangers. My church never had a dull moment during my time there, and they were always open to bringing in traveling ministries that would help impact our city for God. I have a vivid memory of a scene from a guest performance where Jesus shot a flare gun at the devil's belly, and he disappeared into a smoking hole in the stage floor.

When I was eight years old, my church joined forces with a ministry that engaged in a weeklong, live-action drama that carried a heavy-duty shock and awe factor. Members of our church were enlisted to act in the performances. The traveling ministry brought the scary costumes. They titled the event Hell House.

Our church facility underwent a mini-makeover before the Halloween event, and the building looked as though they had hired a psychopath like Dr. Jekyll and Mr. Hyde as their interior designer. I'm surprised nobody else seemed disturbed by the decor choices.

These intense aesthetic adjustments included painting all the interior walls black, staging a crashed motorcycle accident on the side of the gym, parking a hearse outside the front doors of the church as the welcome sign, and turning the Kingdom Kids Sunday School room into the foreboding Gates of Hell.

My family, as well as many church friends, volunteered to act in this dramatic scare-fest. We held hours of rehearsals to ensure our performances would be authentic, haunting, and flawless. I had the pleasure of pretending to witness my own sister's funeral—post car accident. It's bizarre pretending to mourn the loss of your ACTUAL sister, who was lying in a REAL casket. My father acted the role of the preacher who was officiating the funeral service.

Some close family friends from church were involved in a startling scene in the drama where the parents lashed out at each other in furious anger and threatened to get a divorce. Moments later, the teen daughter ran into the bathroom with a knife and began cutting her wrists. This dramatic tour was not for the faint of heart. The weeks of tireless work and preparation culminated in a weeklong, fear-ridden drama for the city of Edmonton.

We acted out these terrifying scenes while groups of curious young adults paraded in groups through the grim crime scenarios and tragedy ensembles, led by a demon-masked skeleton entity who acted as their tour guide

Hell House demonstrated stories of drug overdoses, sickening witchcraft, and hellish torment. These plots are not the usual things churches present in an attempt to increase their attendance.

Once the tour groups successfully made it through the final torments of hell in the Kingdom Kids gym, they were given a breather in a quiet, bland foyer where each person received a tract and was given an opportunity to learn about Jesus and begin a journey with Him. This conclusion to the scary evening was the only redemptive twist on the dramatic, fear-ridden night.

Although Hell House contained elements which could have had a positive impact on some viewers, I saw a conflict of interest in the whole concept.

The use of fear, shock, and horror as a motivator in an attempt to win souls to Christ could have been balanced by portraying His loving care for people, His most valued creation. The nightmarish experience felt like religious terrorism to me! I had trouble sleeping for several weeks due to the shock rock drama. I knew it was an act, and I knew many of the people behind the masks, but the horrifying dramatizations terrified me at a young age. The musky smell of rotten eggs and sulphur from the fiery inferno lingered in the Kingdom Kids hall for weeks after the event.

I think that's how fear works: the more we allow it to flourish and grow, the more it influences our lives with its horrible stench. We face enough fear in our world; the last thing we need is for the family of God to add more terrors.

I wish I could say the fear-mongering was just an isolated incident, only taking place at my church on the west end of town. The troubling truth is that fear is a wide-spread disease, and it does a masterful job of infecting the sanctuaries and neighbourhoods we inhabit.

We were born with God-sized, childlike destinies waiting to be explored. Many times, the enemy attacks our childlike faith, polluting and dismantling it with fear. Whether it's the fear of spending eternity in hell for our bad decisions, or the fear of stepping out into our dreams, this fear often cripples us to the point of standing still, doing nothing useful for the kingdom of God.

We've accepted fear as an unpleasant roommate who must be tolerated continuously but for whom we hold hateful feelings. We can easily fool ourselves into believing that fear is meant to be part of our lives. Jesus talked a lot about how perfect love casts out fear; not some of it or even most of it, but all of it. All the fear, all the time.

We can try to manipulate the fears of others all we want, but it still leaves this same, awful aftertaste in our mouths. It's similar to the effect of chewing mint gum right after taking a swig of Cola. It takes excessive tooth brushing to remove the yucky flavour.

We can't keep fighting the enemy with our earthly, fear-ridden ammunition. Fear cannot be utilized to defeat itself. A flawed mindset states we can beat fear if we battle it with our human effort, but only Jesus holds the keys to help us conquer our fears.

I've read through the Bible a handful of times over the past few years. Some parts I pay more attention to than others. Often, I would read it growing up because my parents or pastor suggested I should. Other times I would read it because I really wanted to. One day, I decided to stop reading the Bible altogether. Instead, I let God's Word read me. God's Word cuts through my walls, my fears, and my false accusations, like a sword cutting through bones and marrow.

One of the first things Jesus read into me was how I was too focused on earthly battles, unaware of the unseen battle which is the real threat to my relationship with Him. I reflected on how I was spending too much time gaining passive knowledge, observing all of the conflicts going on in the world on the evening news, and not spending enough time focusing on a solution.

Jesus offers real hope to those of us who are crippled by fear. Though we may never be completely fearless on this side of eternity, Jesus gives us the courage every day to fear less. He beckons our inner child into unrelenting bravery and courage, while standing in the face of our greatest fears.

The Bible states that God doesn't give us a spirit of fear, but of power, love, and a sound mind. We are no longer slaves to fear because we are accepted into God's family. We are children of God. All I can think about now is how Perfect Love Casts Out All Fear.

Fear seems to sell but I'm not buying it anymore. Jesus never scared anyone into loving Him. Even when He had the opportunity to cast judgements and stones, He decided to lay down His weapon and draw a line in the sand. Maybe it's time for our generation to draw our line in the sand and identify our real enemy: Fear.

ISIS isn't our enemy. Political conflicts aren't our enemy. Human trafficking rings aren't our enemies either. The real enemy is the fear surrounding such unspeakable evil. Fear subsides when it's not on display.

This is why I don't view the evening news anymore.

The news is the world's attempt to teach us to subscribe to fear. From an early age, we are programmed to be afraid.

Fear is a fake weapon the enemy flaunts all day long in an attempt to cripple and defeat our childlike nature before we can step out into our hopeful, childlike destinies. Fear is the fake enemy we need to collectively fight against and abolish for good.

The key word here is FAKE. Fear isn't real. I heard it once said that fear is False Evidence Appearing Real. Fear is the opposite of faith. Faith is putting our confidence in unseen things where hope is the evidence, while fear is a belief in hopeless things with an overwhelming lack of evidence. Simply put, fear is misusing our God-given imaginations. Instead of believing for the near impossible, we let our worries sabotage both our faith in God, and our ability to be victorious in our lives.

I've struggled with a fear-based mindset for years. As a kid, I watched scary movies from the library in an attempt to build up a tolerance to fear. The strategy didn't work. Fear always had the upper hand in my life. I'm also guilty of putting on scary masks in an attempt to manipulate others into faith in God, but I've discovered that tactic is useless. Those who experience fear-based Christianity often end up wanting nothing to do with the church.

It's time to hand out love like Halloween candy, even to the scary, costumed characters wandering the city streets. We need to extend fearless love to the monsters, ghosts, and ghouls who don't even deserve a rotten caramel apple. Fearless love is the only thing I know which carries lasting fire-power against the foreboding evil in our world. It's the only weapon that destroys fear, rather than destroying people. I don't believe in scary people as much is I believe in scared people. Don't let fear sweep your hopes and dreams under the bus.

In an ideal world, I'd love to drop a care package of confetti, balloons and birthday cakes on the deserts of Iraq, and greet the ISIS terrorists with this shocking surprise. When they expect a rainstorm of bombs, they would be greeted with the best childlike birthday party ever. I would enlist a group of elementary kids to draw kind pictures and send translated notes about hope, love, and Jesus to these criminals. They would be reminded what it's like to be childlike again and would recapture those feelings, if only for a few moments.

God would want these terrorists to know that everything they ever assumed about Jesus was dead wrong. It's time to ambush these blood-thirsty warlords with the least likely war tactic the world would ever expect: fearless love.

But we can't stop there. We'll take this celebration to the local prisons, brothels, and to the homeless in our cities. Jesus emphatically intends to remove the fear from our lives and replace it with childlike faith and radical hope. Fear subsides when we take action, and the time to take a risk and move is now!

It's time to show the world we're not afraid anymore. We need to let Jesus repeat to us, "Be not afraid." We need to listen to Him until we're ready to start gently whispering the same message to others. We will let this brave refrain echo through the city streets, to the lost and broken, to the naked and ashamed. We will allow this powerful truth to bring faith to our fears, and radical hope to our hopelessness. We need to subscribe to this kind of childlike programming.

SIXTEEN

Mission Impossible

I used to think being childlike was a season,
but now I know it's a mindset.

I had the privilege of attending an incredible summer camp in junior high. I piled my sleeping bag, backpack, water canteen, and pillow into the back of the family van, and my mother and I drove off onto the dusty back roads of Lac Saint Anne County. Camp Nakamun is nestled against the backdrop of a large forest, on the point of a gorgeous summer cottage lake. The lake appeared crystal clear and beautiful from afar, but as you drew nearer, you could see the blue-green algae slowly building up mucky, thick reserves in the water. I recall frequently itching and scratching myself as I walked back from the lake after swimming.

We pulled up at the campsite and walked up to the main lodge to sign in. The lady at the front counter introduced herself as Care Bear and said I would be joining A-Frame 8 with Hansel, the senior counsellor, and his sidekick, John the Baptist.

My mother and I trekked down the winding path system toward my weeklong home in the A-frame cabins.

I hopped up the front steps as a tall, lanky, blonde fellow came bursting out the door and warmly threw up his left hand to offer me a high-five.

"Hey dude, I'm Hansel. Nice to meet you. What's your name?"

All I could do was stand motionless and stare in shock. He looked exactly like Owen Wilson, the actor from Zoolander!

"What's your name, dude?" he asked again.

"Oh, yeah, umm, I'm Justin," I quietly responded. He laughed enthusiastically and clapped me on the shoulder. "Well, it's sure awesome to meet you, Justin. Welcome to A-Frame 8! We are going to have a blast this week. I sure hope you're ready!"

My mother recited her giant list of safety and self-care instructions. She gave me fifteen emergency contact numbers and a detailed map to the nearest hospital, in the event of an alien invasion or a sprained wrist. I thought it was overkill. I dutifully waved goodbye as she left, and then went into the cabin with a sigh of relief. Now the fun could begin!

After a few minutes, the junior counsellor, John the Baptist, rolled into the cabin—literally. He burst through the door on his unicycle! Could this week get any more awesome? We spent the next half hour falling on our faces and scraping our knees while attempting to balance on the single-wheeled contraption. As the week progressed, our cabin exerted heaps of energy, bravery, and adrenaline at every activity.

To my surprise, the week sped by in a flash, and before I knew it, an epic evening at our last campfire unfolded, full of fun songs and engaging stories from the speaker. We sang some memorable songs with actions and dancing. We laughed as we paraded around the campfire singing "Let Me See Your Funky Chicken." The moon soon came out to greet us, and it was time to head back to the cabins for bed. Hansel said a goodnight prayer and congratulated us on another successful day.

Ten minutes later, as we were dozing off to sleep, the lights suddenly flared on in full force, partially blinding a few of the boys. It reminded me of one of those early morning surprise drills in an army movie.

"Gentlemen, prepare for war! Get on your feet!" Hansel shouted.

Astonished and confused, our adrenal glands began pumping fire through our veins as Hansel explained that we were going to engage in a night game called "Mission Impossible." He cautioned us to tie our shoelaces, wear sweaters and long pants, and leave our flashlights behind. My heart began beating like a bass drum.

Two hundred campers gathered in the open field under the moonlight. Excitement hung thick in the air. I heard a constant murmur of laughter as each camper explained to others how their cabin leaders broke the news to them.

Uncle Lou, one of the senior counsellors, came out with a megaphone and explained the rules of the game. The campers would be facing off against all of the camp staff. The object of the game was for each camper to make it from the campfire all the way to the cookhouse on the opposite side of the camp without getting tackled and tagged by a sneaky counsellor. If we got caught, we would have to start over again. The way to tell if the youth had won the game was for us to dump cups of water on a giant fire in the end zone, and put the flames out before the game ended. The counsellors and staff had to prevent the kids from making it to the end zone to put out the blaze. If the fire persisted to the end of the game, the counsellors would win and lord it over us.

Once everyone understood the rules, the siren blasted through the trees to signal the start of the game, followed by the anthemic song from the Mission Impossible films. A few guys and I planned our attack, hanging low as we flanked the edge of the sandbar near the boathouse. The cabin leaders' flashlights flickered, and blood-curdling screams reverberated in the distance. We snuck up to the Bluebird cabins, which stood in a long row on the south edge of the field, without anyone seeing us. Now, only a hundred metres of open ground and several dozen bloodthirsty adults stood between us and the end zone.

I peered around one of the cabins and surveyed the terrain. A few dark shapes walked by in the distance. We heard constant chatter coming from the field ahead of us. I knew we were outnumbered. I felt my stomach turn as I questioned my plan to make a quick dash for the finish line. After a moment of hesitation, I swallowed the lump in my throat and raced for victory.

Several yells came from the open field. They had spotted me! Flashlights popped on and began bouncing as the cabin leaders charged after me. My legs were pumping frantically, and I could hear the footsteps of a larger-than-life counsellor closing in on me. I knew I had to pick up the pace or I would get squashed in a messy tackle. A large hand swung toward me, but I nimbly dodged. I would not go down without a fight!

I rapidly approached the safe zone and made a

flying leap for the finish line. The two counsellors on my tail groaned as I crossed the line with inches to spare. I fell to the ground panting, my heart racing, enjoying the sweet and much-deserved victory. After a minute to catch my breath, I walked over to a picnic table and filled a styrofoam cup with water.

Embers and sparks flew in every direction as I poured water on the fire. We were inching closer to claiming victory over the camp staff!

My friends and I made it to the end zone several more times that night, but not without receiving our share of surprise attacks from the counsellors. I got tackled and laid out on the field several times over. The repeated counsellor dogpiles bruised my knees as well as my ego.

The counsellors took tackling campers way too seriously. A few kids suffered severe injuries. One kid even got tackled into the murky lake. Maybe the adults were trying to get back at us for the lack of sleep all week.

As the night progressed, we managed to put out the campfire before the siren blared, and we won the game! Cheering and shouting erupted through the field.

My friends and I went home after that week with feelings of pride and childlike faith, ready to take on any challenge set before us.

Summer camp was a wonderful break from my challenging adolescent years. I experienced radical joy and wonder during my weeks at camp. A longing was satisfied in my heart for contagious joy, childlike wonder, and overwhelming hope.

I always felt a disconnect between the abundance of life in Jesus at camp compared to the challenges and setbacks in my life at home. The enemy was clearly at work to steal the joy and wonder from my home life. I struggled and warred in the real world to hold onto the childlike joy I received at camp.

Jesus said how the enemy, the devil, would come and pick on us, attempting to dish out a three-course meal of stealing, death, and destruction in our lives. Jesus explained how He came to help and give us life to the fullest and more abundantly.

I don't think Jesus meant for us to arrive in His abundant fullness of life for a single week out of the year and then lose all of that incredible excitement and enthusiasm when we go back to challenging times and tedious daily rituals for the rest of the year.

What would it look like if we brought the wonder of a week at summer camp back to our doorsteps to thrive in a childlike mindset year-round?

So many people experience these mountaintop experiences with God, but when they move out of that season, their enthusiasm slowly deteriorates through the routines of unexciting activities and work. They become mired in the same negative tendencies and thoughts they started with before they reached the mountaintop. The whimsy and adventure our soul craves are polluted by homework, business deals, and menial activities.

Our lives don't have to look so ordinary anymore, because Jesus came down from heaven to break the deception of our everyday world, and to give us extraordinary hope and wonder. Jesus was full of whimsy, and He executed the greatest childlike heist the world has ever seen. He cheated death and brought us all victoriously back from the grave. He now calls us on to larger than life capers to take the world by storm.

One of my favourite authors, Bob Goff, talks a lot about engaging this life of childlike whimsy, no matter your age. Bob used to be a lawyer, but now he spends much of his time being secretly incredible by sharing God's love and inspiring others to live massive, audacious lives. He builds schools in war-torn places and greets world leaders on Tom Sawyer Island in Disneyland. How's that for a life of whimsy?

Those of us who fight to maintain a childlike heart of playfulness are at war with a real enemy daily. The enemy attacks our childlike hopes, to keep us from engaging this life of whimsy. The enemy, the devil, is desperate to see us lose our childlike faith before we ever get a chance to use it. He intends to see the joy which once reigned in our lives overcome with anxiety and disillusionment. He longs to have us believe that being childlike is a season, not a mindset.

The devil influences the systems of this world to ensure our mindset is far removed from childlike freedom. The enemy is hiding out in the bushes at night like those camp counsellors did, waiting to tackle those of us who tread too close to the borderlines of freedom.

The Bible says the devil is prowling around like a roaring lion, waiting to devour us. The devil is working overtime to ensure we stay in the safe zone called ordinary, and never approach the "extraordinary" that Jesus calls us to.

The devil hates it when heaven's childlike way of thinking invades our flawed mindsets. He despises it when we make peace with our pasts and take that healed resolve to learn and grow beyond our life's circumstances and limitations. Living out of a childlike mindset pours buckets of living water over our adversary's fire.

The enemy's flawed mindset would have us believe, "I'm too old, I'm too broken, I'm too sinful to make a difference or to be used by God." If Jesus is all He says He is, trust you are all He says you are.

The childlike mindset of Jesus says, "I am loved, I am accepted, I am gifted, I am free to live." Let the "I am" of heaven, tower high above the "I'm not" of your current situation. What if we chose to believe that our biggest setbacks in this lifetime could actually be the evidence of God's biggest setups for our future selves? God cares deeply, not only about who we currently are, but about the person we are becoming.

Jesus calls for His friends and followers to be born again like little children, in order to enter the kingdom of heaven. His followers argued how it seemed impossible to crawl back into their mother's womb! Jesus explained, the only way this rebirth is possible, is by laying down our flawed, grown up ways of thinking, and choosing to embrace this childlike perspective of His kingdom. Jesus condemned the religious mindset of the Pharisees, and painted a better picture of what he wanted His friends to embody.

He explained that, if we would lose our old lives, we would surely discover real life. This rebirth is available to all of us, if we choose to let go of our old grown up selves, and embark on a new adventure with God. When we seek out Jesus and His ever expanding kingdom, with all of our hearts and minds, we will surely find it. This mysterious kingdom of God is unveiled inside our hearts.

I used to think God only used famous and influential people to change the world, but now I know He likes to confound the wisdom of the esteemed and use people like you and me.

I've decided to take the bricks and mud the enemy has thrown at me and build a new tree fort. This fort isn't your average tree fort either; it's more like a pirate ship, with lots of balloons for sails, towering high over the bored and stressed-out cities of our world. It resembles the Santa Maria replica pirate ship at the mall that I claimed as my new office.

I want to create room in my life and on board my pirate ship for others who long for a more meaningful life. I don't want curious shoppers to just lean over the rails of the hallways taking photos, while starring at me on my ship. I want other curious onlookers to join me onboard on this whimsical, daring adventure!

I need to spend a lot less time complaining about life's circumstances, and a lot more time planning the next caper with my friends. What if we laid down our accusations and our misunderstandings, and chose to no longer be a victim? We can ask Jesus for fearless, childlike joy to reign over our failures and disappointments.

We are new creations in Jesus. This means we can let our old lives and our old ways of thinking pass away. We can then allow God's childlike spirit to begin writing a new story for our lives. Jesus calls us to throw off anything that hinders or trips us up on our journeys, and to run the race with endurance that He has set apart for us. We were born for victory.

My faith in God has outweighed the chaos swirling around my crazy life. C.S. Lewis once said, "Hardships often prepare ordinary people for extraordinary destinies." This is the truth about all of us, and it can set us free.

I don't want to live a life from which I need a vacation, and I bet nobody else does either. I want to fill in the blanks of the ordinary with extraordinary wonder and enthusiasm. I've learned that a few young adults from the Bible had the guts to shake the whole world.

When society says no, Jesus says go! It's really as simple as that. Part of God's dream for our lives is to help others excavate the caves of our childhoods until we find our inner child in hiding. Allowing our inner child to flourish is where the abundant life begins.

Engaging Jesus in this process helped me heal from a whole world of hurt and lingering pain.

Jesus gives me the confidence I'm still a big kid with even bigger dreams. I have deep gratitude now for the hardships I've experienced, for the pain has allowed me to grow stronger. It's provided a new path to inner peace and abundant joy. I understand the words of the Bible now which say, "The joy of the Lord is my strength."

The world desperately needs dreamers, go-getters, mavericks, and artisans to help change it for the better. It's time to take back a lifetime of pain and heartache and recapture the childlike faith which is rightfully ours.

Many people in our world feel bored and stuck. They need a better way to live. This faith-filled, childlike mindset is focused on overcoming evil with good. Jesus robbed the grave, now we get to rob the world of boredom and hopelessness. Let's bring the wonder back onto centre stage as we climb out of the trenches of our childhoods into the arms of our friend Jesus.

Several summers ago, my friend, Paul Woida, and I drove four hours to Fort McMurray Alberta to play a concert. Our first out of town performance as aspiring record-

ing artists had finally arrived. Both of us had spent countless days locked away in our basements practicing song-
writing and performing. We came up with several covers
and original songs to play for the youth gathering.

As we cruised down the highway, we shared our
dreams for the future. I wasn't very skilled at guitar yet,
but I knew my lyrics carried impactful meaning for others.
Paul was extremely talented at singing and playing his
instruments, and was excited to perform for the young
people.

During our conversation, Paul came to a startling
realization.

"Justin, I just don't see how I can do this. I want to
be a full-time musician and perform all over the world, but
I don't believe in myself enough to do it."

"Paul, I believe in your dreams. You were born for
this. If you don't have the belief in yourself to pursue this
dream, borrow my belief instead!" I told him enthusiastically.

A seed of childlike faith was planted inside my
friend that day, a turning point for his future success. I
chatted with Paul recently about our conversation all those
years ago. He reminded me how he borrowed my belief in
pursuing his dreams. Whenever he was faced with times of
doubt, I would encourage him that he was not alone in his
dreams. I was fighting in his court, and I knew God was
orchestrating a beautiful story through it all.

Over the years, we have enjoyed numerous childlike
escapades together. On one occasion, we invited a few
hundred people to join us on the pirate ship at the mall, to
shoot a music video. This spectacle was an amazing site to
watch. The childlike hopes of those onboard were slowly

being restored. I witnessed joy awakening in everyone present.

As we recently laughed and reminisced, Paul filled me in on his latest musical business trip to Nashville. He humbly shared how his dreams are becoming a reality, and he is grateful for my belief in him all those years ago.

It's a dangerously incredible gift for us to say: "I believe in you" to those around us. Those four words carry a hefty amount of firepower when we speak encouragement over our friends and family. If you don't currently believe in yourself, start by believing in somebody else! Shared belief in each other's dreams is the substance of miracles.

We are armed for battle, but instead of fighting with earthly artillery, we will fight with whimsy and fearless love. When the world tries to sell us bullets, we will fight back with balloons. This love we lavish on others will make them amazed that people like us actually exist! We will bring down the facade of mundane adulthood, as we war with our passions, our wonder, and our childlike faith.

We will sing an anthem of hope to a hurting and restless generation. Let's fill our faith balloons with hope and get airborne together. We will declare a new season of wonder, as we watch others engage daring lives of spontaneous joy with Jesus. We were born to steal back this crazy, messed up, adult world and engage the childlike life with Jesus. Jesus won the fight; we get to bring the balloons.

Welcome to The Childlike Heist!

Acknowledgements

Ever since I was a young boy, I've desired to write books. I'm grateful to have grown up in a home where creativity and imagination were always encouraged. I owe my parents and my sister, Janice, a great deal of gratitude and respect for continually encouraging and challenging me to keep fighting for my dreams and to pursue creative possibilities.

I've met some incredible people along the way who have had a tremendous impact on my story. These are the kinds of people you write into memoirs when you find the words to say what they mean to you and how they made you feel.

Thank you to my Lord and Saviour Jesus Christ; You are the reason I live and can write with enthusiasm and vision. Thank you for Your grace and unrelenting mercies. Reading Your Good Book is a limitless well of ideas for writing. I'm forever grateful for all You are and continue to do through me.

A special thank you to Josh and Kiri Erb, for demonstrating the kingdom in action throughout your lives and ministry. You have impacted my life in such profound ways. You've taught me to embrace the adventure of life God calls us to. For that, I'm truly grateful.

To Mark and Sue Wiesinger, and to my wonderful cousins—Josh, Sheena, Jesse, Josie, Mitch and the new cousin-in-laws Zach, Elliot, and Sissel—I'm so grateful for the fond memories we shared together in Australia as I finished writing this book. Being around your family and partaking in your wisdom and childlike joy in the Father has helped inspire much of my writing and passion for God. You've taught me so much about loving people well, sitting on God's knee in times of trouble, and living life to its fullest potential.

To my dear friend, Paul Woida, thank you for being a true brother, close friend, and compadre in my life. I deeply value our time together, and I'm so thrilled we have encouraged each other to step out and take hold of our dreams and passions. I couldn't have written this book without your support.

I need to give a warm shoutout to my wonderful editor, Christine Stobbe. You brought the best out in me throughout the editing process. You challenged me to grow as a writer. Thank you for your constructive criticism and unrelenting effort in this project. I am deeply grateful for working with you on this book.

Thank you to my dear friends from Hope City Church and Gateway Family Church. You have walked alongside me during this writing journey. Thank you to Pastor Phil Kniesel and Pastor Landon Dorsche for communicating love, hope, and encouragement through our every interaction. Thank you to the incredible staff team at Hope City Church for fostering an atmosphere of friendship, joy, and radical hope.

Thank you to my friends for your warm words, prayer, last minute coffee dates, and childlike joy. May the message of this book far exceed anything we had ever expected or envisioned.

May the God of Peace guide you all as you embrace the Childlike Heist that He is beckoning us into.

About the Author

Justin is the only person in Edmonton to have an office on a pirate ship, though he encourages others to join him on his creative exploits when he is planted there with his eye patch, sword, and bubble gum, planning his next caper.

He works as the Media Director at Hope City Church in Edmonton, Alberta, where he uses the medium of film to tell stories and communicate the church's vision and weekly events.

Justin is driven by a desire to see people of all ages discover and thrive in their God-given creative destinies. He is building a creative ministry team of young people at his church, discipling and teaching video production and storytelling. His dream is to see his church become a beacon of light and an outpost of creative arts in Canada and around the world.

Justin has begun a grassroots creative arts conference for young people called Innovate + Create in his city. His friend, Paul Woida, co-hosts the event. They give in-depth workshops on filmmaking, entrepreneurship, and all things music.

Justin is the proud owner of Intrinsic Media Group, where he films music videos and other exciting projects with his small team of fellow creatives. He is excited to see young people across Edmonton and abroad explore and experience the power of kingdom creativity, while learning how God can intersect their lives and stories in unique and incredible ways.

Connect with Justin

Justin loves doing life with people everywhere. He rarely schedules daily routines because he plans to be accessible to others when they need him.

He is available to teach and inspire people of all ages to take back their God-given childlike wonder and to approach life with zeal, determination, and radical hope. Justin brings his unique perspective on engaging our lives with Jesus and communicating through the use of hilarious and inspiring stories and memorable life lessons.

If you would like to have Justin speak at your event or gathering, you can reach him here:
email: thechildlikeheist@gmail.coom

If you are in need of a friend, or someone to listen, Justin does that too.

He can be reached here:
Instagram: @Justintowriting
Twitter: @JustinWiesinger

You can also read his blog at: justintowriting.com